THE WORDS OF
PEACE

SELECTIONS FROM THE SPEECHES
OF THE WINNERS
OF THE NOBEL PEACE PRIZE

Selected and edited by Irwin Abrams,
Distinguished University Professor Emeritus,
Antioch University

Foreword by
President Jimmy Carter

Newmarket Press
New York

90 91 92 93   10 9 8 7 6 5 4 3 2 1 HC

Library of Congress Cataloging-in-Publication Data
The words of peace : selections from the speeches of the winners of the Nobel Peace Prize / selected and edited by Irwin Abrams : foreword by President Jimmy Carter.
   p.   cm.
   ISBN 1-55704-060-5
   1. Peace. 2. Peace—Awards. 3. Nobel prizes. I. Abrams, Irwin. 1914– .
JX1963.W713 1990
327.1′72—dc20   90-5851
                                         CIP

Quantity Purchases
Companies, professional groups, clubs, and other organizations may qualify for special terms when ordering quantities of this title. For information, write to Special Sales Department, Newmarket Press, 18 East 48th Street, New York, N.Y. 10017, or call (212) 832-3575.

CONTENTS

10/2/91 PEC/KA

Egyptian President Anwar el-Sadat (left) *and Israeli Prime Minister Menachem Begin* (right) *with President Jimmy Carter at the White House (1978).*

FOREWORD

"In our private and individual lives, all of us have a need to seek for heroes. In our own personal ambitions and life—analysis of what opportunities present themselves to us, the talents that we have, the unpredictable future—we need those on whom we can depend as a pattern. How can we live an exemplary existence? The measurement of that, the pattern for it, the guide for our own lives, comes from our heroes. How can we justify our dreams? How can we confirm our beliefs? How can we prove to ourselves that what we have been taught as children is true? How can we alleviate our doubts? How can we, in our own often naturally dormant lives, be inspired to action, sometimes even at the sacrifice of our own immediate well-being? We derive those inspirations from heroes."

These are my considered thoughts about heroes, presented in a speech in 1986. The Nobel Peace Prize was established to honor the heroes of peace, and this small book presents a collection of well-chosen excerpts from their addresses at Oslo, drawn both from acceptance speeches and from the lectures which each prize winner is expected to deliver.

The heroes of peace whose words are to be found here have followed a variety of paths toward their goal. Alfred Nobel had specified in his will that his prize was to be given for the organizing of peace congresses and efforts for disarmament, but also for work for "fraternity between nations." Beginning with the very first prize in 1901, the Norwegian Nobel Committee has used the last phrase to interpret peacemaking ever more broadly.

While the majority of the early prizes went to peace activists, such as Nobel's friend Baroness Bertha von Suttner, prizes have been given away to many statesmen. The first of these went to President Theodore Roosevelt in 1906 for his role in negotiating an end to the Russo-Japanese War. Most recently, President Oscar Arias Sánchez won the prize in 1987 for his Central American Peace Plan, which has since contributed so much to bringing peace to that troubled area. I am especially happy to find represented in this volume my collaborators in the peacemaking of Camp David, Menachem Begin and Anwar Sadat, who was to die so tragically as a martyr to those efforts.

Heroes of peace to be found in these pages represent a great diversity: leaders of Red Cross organizations, whose work in the midst of violence has testified to the existence of the bonds of humanity; great humanitarians like Fridtjof Nansen and his successors in the Office of the United Nations High Commissioner for Refugees, who have sought to care for the millions who have been uprooted from their homeland in this war-torn century; others, such as Albert Schweitzer and Mother Teresa, whose acts of charity were inspired by their deep religious faith; religious leaders like Archbishop Söderblom and the Dalai Lama of Tibet, who emphasized that peace must first come to the human heart; scientists like Lord Boyd-Orr and Norman Borlaug, who worked for peace by bringing more food to a hungry world; other scientists like Linus Pauling, Evgeny Chazov, and Bernard Lown, who tried to prevent the nuclear catastrophe that their science told them might end life on this planet; apostles of disarmament like Philip Noel-Baker and Alva Myrdal; practitioners of nonviolence, such as the Quakers and the Peace People of Northern Ireland; and United Nations peacemakers, such as Ralph Bunche and Pérez de Cuéllar.

I have been happy to see the prize given more frequently in recent years to champions of human rights, who have a special section in this book. They include opponents of apartheid in South Africa, Chief Albert Lutuli and Archbishop Desmond

Tutu; Martin Luther King, Jr., who fought and died for civil rights for all North Americans; Pérez Esquivel, who was imprisoned and tortured for his peace witness in Argentina; Andrei Sakharov, who lived just long enough to see his sacrifices for human rights begin to bear fruit in the Soviet Union; Lech Walesa, who led the struggle for workers' rights in Poland; Elie Wiesel, who will not let the world forget the atrocities wreaked on human beings in the Holocaust; and the leaders of Amnesty International, who defend the rights of prisoners of conscience throughout the world.

I am convinced that for peace to endure, it must encompass justice, and I am confident that we can perceive today an inexorable trend toward the enhancement of human rights.

We need many kinds of peacemakers. We need those who work to resolve civil wars and international conflicts. We also need those who can establish ways to control and to reduce armaments. Preventing nuclear holocaust remains the highest priority.

We must also work to establish social and political conditions in which all human beings can enjoy freedom and the fullest measure of happiness. I think of those who struggle nonviolently for human rights, those who fight disease and poverty and hunger, and those who work to improve and preserve our environment. But even these efforts to build sound foundations for peace are in themselves not enough. Nobel's "fraternity between nations," the spirit of human brotherhood, must undergird any political or social structure of peace if it is to last. Archbishop Söderblom refers to this in these pages as the "soul" of such a structure; Albert Schweitzer speaks of it here as "the ethical spirit."

I have seen this spirit at work in men and women of myriad religious faiths and philosophical beliefs. I have found it in the volunteers of Habitat for Humanity, with whom Rosalynn and

I have erected homes for the homeless. I have found it in the heroes I have come to know as the recipients of the human rights prize which Mrs. Dominique de Menil and I have established. And I have found it in world leaders like my martyred friend President Sadat.

Many of the heroes of peace who speak to us in these pages have spoken far more vibrantly in their deeds, motivated by this spirit. As we have found inspiration in their work for peace, so may we find inspiration in this excellent collection of their "Words of Peace."

PRESIDENT JIMMY CARTER
The Carter Presidential Center
Atlanta, Georgia
March, 1990

INTRODUCTION

In 1991 it will be ninety years since the first Peace Prize was awarded. The years that have followed that award have not been very peaceful. It can be said that the twentieth century has been one of the most warlike centuries in Western history. Alfred Nobel would certainly have been disappointed if he had lived to see what came to happen in Europe: two bloody world wars and armament build-ups with incredibly destructive weapons. Have all his hopes for a peaceful world proved to be an illusion? I think it is more correct to say that Alfred Nobel was ahead of his time. If he had lived today, he would have been even more engaged in work for peace. And he would have seen that the idea of peace has much stronger support today than ninety years ago—in spite of, or rather because of, what has happened since he wrote his last will.

Peace is first of all the absence of war between states. That means that an international state dominated by power politics has to be replaced by an international system that makes it possible to resolve conflicts by means other than the use of arms. It has been a central task for peace workers to establish a system based on international law and peaceful solutions to conflicts—an aim strongly supported by two great American presidents, Woodrow Wilson and Franklin D. Roosevelt.

The Peace Prizes that have been awarded tell us, however, that peace means more than just the absence of war. Peace is also the absence of suppression and injustice. When people live with suppression, hunger, and lack of any hope for the future, conflicts will arise and the chance of war increases. Only international solidarity with people living under unjust conditions can create a more peaceful world.

In later years the Norwegian Nobel Committee, through its awards, has stressed the importance of human rights and justice.

Equality between different races has been stressed through awards to Albert Lutuli, Martin Luther King, Jr., and Desmond Tutu. The prizes to Andrei Sakharov and Lech Walesa mark a protest against the suppression of human rights in authoritarian societies. It has been encouraging to see that what has occurred in the last years in the field of human rights has been in the direction that these awards have tried to stimulate.

There will almost always be controversy connected with the award of the Peace Prizes. There is a wide spectrum of very different ideas on the question of what measures will best serve the cause of peace. And when the Prize is awarded to a fighter for human rights, the Nobel Committee is often accused of interfering in the domestic affairs of other states. It is an international concern in the same way as the struggle against poverty and the threat against our environment are concerns for the whole international community. We are rapidly moving in a direction where we have to find international solutions to the problems we are facing.

The Nobel prize winners have an obligation to deliver the Nobel lecture. The lecture is usually presented the day after the Peace Prize ceremony. It is also now customary that the prize winner, during the ceremony, makes a short speech of thanks. In the lecture and speech, the winner has an opportunity to present ideas on what he or she thinks are the most important peace issues we are facing. Their thoughts are well documented in the selections Professor Irwin Abrams has carefully chosen for this book.

The struggle for peace goes on continuously. Willy Brandt tells us something very important in a few sentences: "Peace, like freedom, is no original state which existed from the start; we shall have to make it, in the truest sense of the word."

PROFESSOR JAKOB SVERDRUP
The Norwegian Nobel Institute
Oslo, Norway
March, 1990

PEACE

"The stars of eternal truth and right have always shone in the firmament of human understanding. The process of bringing them down to earth, remolding them into practical forms, imbuing them with vitality, and then making use of them has been a long one.

"One of the eternal truths is that happiness is created and developed in peace, and one of the eternal rights is the individual's right to live. The strongest of all instincts, that of self-preservation, is an assertion of this right, affirmed and sanctified by the ancient commandment: Thou shalt not kill."

—BERTHA VON SUTTNER (1905)*

"The adherents of the old order have a powerful ally in the natural law of inertia inherent in humanity which is, as it were, a natural defense against change. Thus pacifism faces no easy struggle. This question of whether violence or law shall prevail between states is the most vital of the problems of our eventful era, and the most serious in its repercussions. The beneficial results of a secure world peace are almost inconceivable, but even

---

*The italicized date at the end of each selection and in the biographical entries represents the year for which the prize was awarded; on several occasions the Nobel Committee postponed its decision for a certain year and then made the grant of that year's prize one year later. The selections have been excerpted both from the acceptance speeches and from the lectures delivered by the prize winners.

more inconceivable are the consequences of the threatening world war which many misguided people are prepared to precipitate. The advocates of pacifism are well aware how meager are their resources of personal influence and power. They know that they are still few in number and weak in authority, but when they realistically consider themselves and the ideal they serve, they see themselves as the servants of the greatest of all causes."

—*BERTHA VON SUTTNER* *(1905)*

"Man's greatest advances these last few generations have been made by the application of human intelligence to the management of matter. Now we are confronted by a more difficult problem, the application of intelligence to the management of human relations. Unless we can advance in that field also, the very instruments that man's intelligence has created may be the instruments of his destruction.

"The obstacles to peace are not obstacles in matter, in inanimate nature, in the mountains which we pierce, in the seas across which we fly. The obstacles to peace are in the minds and hearts of men.

"In the study of matter we can be honest, impartial, true. That is why we succeed in dealing with it. But about the things we care for—which are ourselves, our desires and lusts, our patriotisms and hates—we find a harder test of thinking straight and truly. Yet there is the greater need. Only by intellectual rectitude and in that field shall we be saved. There is no refuge but in truth, in human intelligence, in the unconquerable mind of man."

—*NORMAN ANGELL* *(1933)*

"Not long before the war the familiar doctrine was stated by a British cabinet minister at a great meeting in Manchester in some such terms as these: 'There is just one way in which we may have peace and be secure; and that is to be so much stronger than any potential enemy that he will not dare attack us. This I submit is a self-evident proposition.'

"Whereupon a thousand or so hardheaded business men of Manchester cheered to the echo. The proposition they were cheering was that two nations likely to quarrel would keep the peace and be secure when each was stronger than the other. It is possible that most, on second thoughts, would be brought to see that the principle does indeed defy arithmetic, but the vast majority would be sincerely astonished if it were suggested that this method of defense also defies morals, is based upon a flat denial of right, in the sense that each denies to the other the right he claims for himself.

"By that policy a nation, in order to be secure in its defense, has to be stronger than its potential enemy. Then what becomes of the defense of that other? Is he to have none?"

—*NORMAN ANGELL* *(1933)*

"A dark and terrible side of this sense of community of interests is the fear of a horrible common destiny which in these days of atomic weapons darkens men's minds all around the globe. Men have a sense of being subject to the same fate, of being all in the same boat. But fear is a poor motive to which to appeal, and I am sure that 'peace people' are on a wrong path when they expatiate on the horrors of a new world war. Fear weakens the nerves and distorts the judgment. It is not by fear that mankind must exorcise the demon of destruction and cruelty, but by motives more reasonable, more humane, and more heroic."

—*EMILY GREENE BALCH* (1946)

"If the target of output were the satisfaction of human needs, there would be no difficulty about markets. When the United States was battling with unemployment, the late President Roosevelt said that there were so many people ill-fed, ill-clothed, and ill-housed that if their needs were to be satisfied, there would be work for every man and woman willing to work. If that were true of the United States, how much truer is it of the world in which two out of every three people suffer premature death for the lack of the primary necessities of life. The upsurge in Asia, which is liable to spread to all colored races, is fundamentally a revolt against hunger and poverty. There can be no peace in the world so long as a large proportion of the population lacks the necessities of life and believes that a change of the political and

economic system will make them available. World peace must be based on world plenty."
—*JOHN BOYD-ORR* (1949)

"Peace is no mere matter of men fighting or not fighting. Peace, to have meaning for many who have known only suffering in both peace and war, must be translated into bread or rice, shelter, health, and education, as well as freedom and human dignity—a steadily better life. If peace is to be secure, long-suffering and long-starved, forgotten peoples of the world, the underprivileged and the undernourished, must begin to realize without delay the promise of a new day and a new life."
—*RALPH J. BUNCHE* (1950)

"There will be no security in our world, no release from agonizing tension, no genuine progress, no enduring peace, until, in Shelley's fine words, 'reason's voice, loud as the voice of nature, shall have waked the nations.' "
—*RALPH J. BUNCHE* (1950)

Ralph Bunche, Undersecretary of the United Nations, with his family as he leaves from New York for the Congo to oversee UN operations there (1963).

"Defeatism about the future is a crime. The danger is not in trying to do too much, but in trying to do too little. [Fridtjof] Nansen said here in 1926 that 'in the big things of life, it is vitally important to leave no line of retreat. . . . We must destroy the bridges behind us which lead back to the old policy and the old system, both of which are such utter failures.'

"In the age when the atom has been split, the moon encircled, diseases conquered, is disarmament so difficult a matter that it must remain a distant dream? To answer 'Yes' is to despair of the future of mankind."

—PHILIP NOEL-BAKER (1959)

"All that I have said boils down to the point of affirming that mankind's survival is dependent upon man's ability to solve the problems of racial injustice, poverty, and war; the solution of these problems is in turn dependent upon man's squaring his moral progress with his scientific progress, and learning the practical art of living in harmony."

—MARTIN LUTHER KING, JR. (1964)

"The destiny of world civilization depends upon providing a decent standard of living for all mankind. The guiding principles of the recipient of the 1969 Nobel Peace Price, the International Labor Organization, are expressed in its charter words, 'Universal and lasting peace can be established only if it is based upon social justice. If you desire peace, cultivate justice.' This is magnificent; no one can disagree with this lofty principle.

"Almost certainly, however, the first essential component of social justice is adequate food for all mankind. Food is the moral right of all who are born into this world. Yet today fifty percent of the world's population goes hungry. Without food, man can live at most but a few weeks; without it, all other components of social justice are meaningless. Therefore I feel that the aforementioned guiding principle must be modified to read: If you desire peace, cultivate justice, but at the same time cultivate the fields to produce more bread; otherwise there will be no peace."

—*NORMAN BORLAUG* *(1970)*

"Peace, like freedom, is no original state which existed from the start; we shall have to make it, in the truest sense of the word."

—*WILLY BRANDT* *(1971)*

"Peace is something more than the absence of war, although some nations would be thankful for that alone

today. A durable and equitable peace system requires
equal development opportunities for all nations."
—*WILLY BRANDT* *(1971)*

"If the attainment of peace is the ultimate objective of
all statesmen, it is, at the same time, something very or-
dinary, closely tied to the daily life of each individual. In
familiar terms, it is the condition that allows each individual and his family to pursue, without fear, the purpose of their lives. It is only in such circumstances that
each individual will be able to devote himself, without
the loss of hope for the future of mankind, to the education of his children, to an attempt to leave upon the history of mankind the imprint of his own creative and
constructive achievements in the arts, culture, religion,
and other activities fulfilling social aspirations. This is the
peace which is essential for all individuals, peoples, nations, and thus for the whole of humanity."
—*EISAKU SATO* *(1974)*

"To the whole world, we repeat the same message that
we proclaimed in August 1976. It is the Declaration of
the Peace People:
'We have a simple message for the world from this
movement for peace.

'We want to live and love and build a just and peaceful society.

'We want for our children, as we want for ourselves, lives at home, at work and at play to be lives of joy and peace.

'We recognize that to build such a life demands of all of us dedication, hard work and courage.

'We recognize that there are many problems in our society which are a source of conflict and violence.

'We recognize that every bullet fired and every exploding bomb makes that work more difficult.

'We reject the use of the bomb and the bullet and all the techniques of violence.

'We dedicate ourselves to working with our neighbors, near and far, day in and day out, to building that peaceful society in which the tragedies we have known are a bad memory and a continuing warning.' "

—*BETTY WILLIAMS* (1976)

"Peace is the beauty of life. It is sunshine. It is the smile of a child, the love of a mother, the joy of a father, the togetherness of a family. It is the advancement of man, the victory of a just cause, the triumph of truth. Peace is all of these and more and more.

"But in my generation, Ladies and Gentlemen, there was a time indescribable. Six million Jews—men, women and children—a number larger than many a nation in Europe—were dragged to a wanton death and slaughtered methodically in the heart of the civilized continent. . . . Those who were doomed, deprived of their

human dignity, starved, humiliated, led away and ultimately turned into ashes cried out for rescue—but in
vain.

"At such a time, unheard of since the first generation,
the hour struck to rise and fight—for the dignity of man,
for survival, for liberty, for every value of the human
image a man has been endowed with by his Creator, for
every known inalienable right he stands for and lives for.
Indeed, there are days when to fight for a cause so abso-
lutely just is the hardest human command. Norway has
known such days, and so have we. Only in honoring that
command comes the regeneration of the concept of
peace. You rise, you struggle, you make sacrifices to
achieve and guarantee the prospect of hope of living in
peace—for you and your people, for your children and
their children.

"Let it, however, be declared and known, stressed, and
noted that fighters for freedom hate war. . . . This is our
common maxim and belief—that if through your efforts
and sacrifices you win liberty and with it the prospect of
peace, then work for peace because there is no mission
in life more sacred."

—*MENACHEM BEGIN* *(1978)*

"I repeat what I said in the Knesset more than a year
ago:

'Any life lost in war is the life of a human being, irrespective of whether it is an Arab or an Israeli.

'The wife who becomes widowed is a human being,
entitled to live in a happy family, Arab or Israeli.

'Innocent children, deprived of paternal care and sympathy, are all our children, whether they live on Arab or Israeli soil, and we owe them the biggest responsibility of providing them with a happy present and bright future.

'For the sake of all this, for the sake of protecting the lives of all our sons and brothers:

'For our societies to produce in security and confidence:

'For the development of man, his well-being and his right to share in an honorable life:

'For our responsibility toward the coming generations:

'For the smile of every child born on our land.' "

—*MOHAMMED ANWAR EL-SADAT* *(1978)*

" 'Peace is more than just absence of war. It is rather a state in which no people of any country, in fact no group of people of any kind live in fear or in need. . . .' Today, more than ten million refugees live in fear or in need. On our road towards a better future for mankind we certainly cannot ignore the tragic presence of those millions for whom peace does not exist. Whenever we solve one single problem we have contributed to peace for the individual. Whenever we bring peace to the individual we are making our world a slightly better place in which to live."

—*POUL HARTLING,* representing the Office of the United Nations High Commissioner for Refugees, and quoting from the 1954 speech of Dr. G. Jan van Heuven Goedhart *(1981)*

"Peace is not a matter of prizes or trophies. It is not the product of a victory or command. It has no finishing line, no final deadline, no fixed definition of achievement.

"Peace is a never-ending process, the work of many decisions by many people in many countries. It is an attitude, a way of life, a way of solving problems and resolving conflicts. It cannot be forced on the smallest nation or enforced by the largest. It cannot ignore our differences or overlook our common interests. It requires us to work and live together."

—*OSCAR ARIAS SÁNCHEZ* *(1987)*

"Peace consists, very largely, in the fact of desiring it with all one's soul. The inhabitants of my small country, Costa Rica, have realized those words by Erasmus. Mine is an unarmed people, whose children have never seen a fighter or a tank or a warship."

—*OSCAR ARIAS SÁNCHEZ* *(1987)*

"My country is a country of teachers. It is therefore a country of peace. We discuss our successes and failures in complete freedom. Because our country is a country of teachers, we closed the army camps, and our children go about with books under their arms, not with rifles on their shoulders. We believe in dialogue, in agreement, in reaching a consensus."

—*OSCAR ARIAS SÁNCHEZ* *(1987)*

"Peace—the word evokes the simplest and most cherished dream of humanity. Peace is, and has always been, the ultimate human aspiration. And yet our history overwhelmingly shows that while we speak incessantly of peace, our actions tell a very different story.

"Peace is an easy word to say in any language. As Secretary-General of the United Nations, I hear it so frequently, from so many different mouths and different sources, that it sometimes seems to me to be a general incantation more or less deprived of practical meaning. What do we really mean by peace?

"Human nature being what it is, peace must inevitably be a relative condition. The essence of life is struggle and competition, and to that extent perfect peace is an almost meaningless abstraction. Struggle and competition are stimulating, but when they degenerate into conflict it is usually both destructive and disruptive. The aim of political institutions like the United Nations is to draw the line between struggle and conflict and to make it possible for nations to stay on the right side of that line. . . .

"These [peace-keeping forces] are soldiers without enemies. Their duty is to remain above the conflict. They may only use their weapons in the last resort for self-defense. Their strength is that, representing the will of the international community, they provide an honorable alternative to war and a useful pretext for peace. Their presence is often the essential prerequisite for negotiating a settlement. They have, or should have, a direct connection with the process of peacemaking."

—*JAVIER PÉREZ DE CUÉLLAR,*
representing the United Nations
Peace-Keeping Forces *(1988)*

"Peace, in the sense of the absence of war, is of little value to someone who is dying of hunger or cold. It will not remove the pain of torture inflicted on a prisoner of conscience. It does not comfort those who have lost their loved ones in floods caused by senseless deforestation in a neighboring country. Peace can only last where human rights are respected, where the people are fed, and where individuals and nations are free."

— *THE DALAI LAMA* *(1989)*

"Peace starts within each one of us. When we have inner peace, we can be at peace with those around us. When our community is in a state of peace, it can share that peace with neighboring communities, and so on. When we feel love and kindness towards others, it not only makes others feel loved and cared for, but it helps us also to develop inner happiness and peace."

— *THE DALAI LAMA* *(1989)*

Albert Schweitzer talking with a patient at his hospital near Lambarene, Gabon (1963).

THE
BONDS
OF
HUMANITY

"If a present-day prophet were to exhort the peoples to peace and common sense, he would speak as one human being to others. With the power of the law and the gentleness of the Gospel, he would speak thus: 'Patriotism is a noble feeling, insofar as it approaches that which is purely human, but the very reverse the further it is removed therefrom. No interests, however great, are higher than those common to the whole of mankind. Among them, the foremost is the old commandment, as old as the oldest documents of any nation: Thou shalt not kill! You are all of one blood. Love one another. People can. Nations can. All this is eminently possible because love is as natural as national hatred is the most unnatural of all human feelings.'"

—*KLAS PONTUS ARNOLDSON* *(1908)*

"But more important by far than any political disarmament of armies and fleets is the 'disarmament' of the people from within, the generation, in fact, of sympathy in the souls of men."

—*FRIDTJOF NANSEN* *(1922)*

"The festival of Christmas is approaching, when the message to mankind is: Peace on earth.

"Never has suffering and bewildered mankind awaited

the Prince of Peace with greater longing, the Prince of Charity who holds aloft a white banner bearing the one word inscribed in golden letters: 'Work.'

"All of us can become workers in his army on its triumphant march across the earth to raise a new spirit in a new generation—to bring men love of their fellow-men and an honest desire for peace—to bring back the will to work and the joy of work—to bring faith in the dawn of a new day."

—*FRIDTJOF NANSEN* (1922)

"To contrast national solidarity and international cooperation as two opposites seems foolish to me. As Germany's representative in Geneva, I expressed the belief that it cannot have been intended in the divine plan that man's noblest abilities should be working in opposition to one another. I tried to make the point that the man who cultivates to the highest degree the qualities inherent in his national culture will gain insight into universal knowledge and feeling which transcend the limitations of his own heritage; and he will create works which, like cathedrals, although built upon the soil of his native land, will soar into the heaven of all mankind. A Shakespeare could have arisen only on English soil. In the same way, your great dramatists and poets express the nature and essence of the Norwegian people, but they also express that which is universally valid for all mankind. . . . National culture can act as a bridge, instead of an obstacle, to mutual spiritual and intellectual understanding. The great men of a nation reach out to all mankind. They are unifying, not divisive; internationally conciliating and still great nationally."

—*GUSTAV STRESEMANN* (1926)

"The policy I have endeavored to sketch is big, bold, and far-reaching. It will be no light and simple task to lay the foundations of a World Commonwealth. It is, on the contrary, perhaps, the greatest and most difficult enterprise ever imagined by the audacious mind of man. But it is a task which has become a necessity. It is an enterprise that is solidly grounded in realities and in the facts of the modern world. If there is still virtue in our common Western civilization and our faith in democracy—and I believe there is—then we must dare to announce that policy as a challenge to the world and as the summons to a great crusade for peace. What greater cause and what more splendid adventure can be set before the youth of the world than the endeavor to bring into being that age-old dream of saints and sages—the great Commonwealth of the World as the visible embodiment of the brotherhood of man?"

—*ARTHUR HENDERSON* (1934)

"The common people of all nations want peace. In the presence of great impersonal forces they feel individually helpless to promote it. You are saying to them here today that common folk, not statesmen, nor generals,

Gustav Stresemann, appointed the German foreign minister in 1924, hastened Germany's entry into the League of Nations.

nor great men of affairs, but just simple plain men and women like the few thousand Quakers and their friends, if they devote themselves to resolute insistence on goodwill in place of force, even in the face of great disaster past or threatened, can do something to build a better, peaceful world. The future hope of peace lies with such personal sacrificial service. To this ideal humble persons everywhere may contribute."

> —*HENRY J. CADBURY,* representing the American Friends Service Committee *(1947)*

"The spirit is not dead; it lives in isolation. It has overcome the difficulty of having to exist in a world out of harmony with its ethical character. It has come to realize that it can find no home other than in the basic nature of man. . . .

"It is convinced that compassion, in which ethics takes root, does not assume its true proportions until it embraces not only man but every living being. To the old ethics, which lacked this depth and force of conviction, has been added the ethics of reverence for life, and its validity is steadily gaining in recognition."

> —*ALBERT SCHWEITZER* *(1952)*

"Their [the League of Nations' and the United Nations'] efforts were doomed to fail since they were obliged to undertake them in a world in which there was no prevailing spirit directed toward peace. And being only legal institutions, they were unable to create such a spirit. The ethical spirit alone has the power to generate it. Kant deceived himself in thinking that he could dispense with it in his search for peace. We must follow the road on which he turned his back."

—*ALBERT SCHWEITZER* (1952)

"Is the spirit capable of achieving what we in our distress must expect of it?

"Let us not underestimate its power, the evidence of which can be seen throughout the history of mankind. The spirit created this humanitarianism which is the origin of all progress toward some form of higher existence. Inspired by humanitarianism we are true to ourselves and capable of creating. Inspired by a contrary spirit we are unfaithful to ourselves and fall prey to all manner of error."

—*ALBERT SCHWEITZER* (1952)

"But Kant's reliance on the people's innate love for peace has not been justified. Because the will of the people, being the will of the crowd, has not avoided the danger of instability and the risk of emotional distraction from the path of true reason, it has failed to demonstrate a vital sense of responsibility. Nationalism of the worst sort was displayed in the last two wars, and it may be

regarded today as the greatest obstacle to mutual understanding between peoples.

"Such nationalism can be repulsed only through the
rebirth of a humanitarian ideal among men which will
make their allegiance to their country a natural one inspired by genuine ideals. . . .

"All men, even the semicivilized and the primitive,
are, as beings capable of compassion, able to develop a
humanitarian spirit. It abides within them like tinder
ready to be lit, waiting only for a spark."

—ALBERT SCHWEITZER (1952)

"I am well aware that what I have had to say on the
problem of peace is not essentially new. It is my profound conviction that the solution lies in our rejecting
war for an ethical reason; namely, that war makes us
guilty of the crime of inhumanity. . . .

"The only originality I claim is that for me this truth
goes hand in hand with the intellectual certainty that the
human spirit is capable of creating in our time a new
mentality, an ethical mentality. Inspired by this certainty,
I too proclaim this truth in the hope that my testimony
may help to prevent its rejection as an admirable senti-
ment but a practical impossibility. Many a truth has lain
unnoticed for a long time, ignored simply because no
one perceived its potential for becoming reality.

"Only when an ideal of peace is born in the minds of
the peoples will the institutions set up to maintain this
peace effectively fulfill the function expected of them."

—ALBERT SCHWEITZER (1952)

"There can be no real peace in this world as long as hundreds of thousands of men, women and children, through no fault of their own, but only because they sacrificed all they possessed for the sake of what they believed, still remain in camps and live in misery and in the greatest uncertainty of their future. Eventually, if we wait too long, the uprooted are bound to become easy prey for political adventurers, from whom the world has suffered too much already. Before anything of that sort happens, let us join our hands in an all-out effort to solve their problem.

"Many years ago I participated in a discussion on the problem of international education. After many experts had presented their complicated theories, an old headmaster of a certain school got up and quietly said: 'There is only one system of education, through love and one's own example.' He was right. What is true for education is true also for the refugee problem of today. With love and our own example—example in the sense of sacrifice—it can be solved. And if in the cynical times in which we live someone might be inclined to laugh at 'love' and 'example' as factors in politics, he would do well to be reminded of Nansen's hard-hitting, direct, and courageous words, based on a life full of sacrifice and devotion: 'Love of man is practical policy.' "

—DR. G. JAN VAN HEUVEN
GOEDHART, representing the Office of
United Nations Commissioner for
Refugees (1954)

"That problem, why men fight who aren't necessarily fighting men, was posed for me in a new and dramatic way one Christmas Eve in London during World War II. The air raid sirens had given their grim and accustomed warning. Almost before the last dismal moan had ended, the anti-aircraft guns began to crash. In between their bursts I could hear the deeper, more menacing sound of bombs. It wasn't much of a raid, really, but one or two of the bombs seemed to fall too close to my room. I was reading in bed and, to drown out or at least to take my mind off the bombs, I reached out and turned on the radio. I was fumbling aimlessly with the dial when the room was flooded with the beauty and peace of Christmas carol music. Glorious waves of it wiped out the sound of war and conjured up visions of happier peacetime Christmases. Then the announcer spoke—in German—for it was a German station and they were Germans who were singing those carols. Nazi bombs screaming through the air with their message of war and death; German music drifting through the air with its message of peace and salvation. When we resolve the paradox of those two sounds from a single national source, we will, at last, be in a good position to understand and solve the problem of peace and war."

—*LESTER B. PEARSON* *(1957)*

"Let us be wary of mass solutions, let us be wary of statistics. We must love our neighbors as ourselves. . . . There is perhaps no surer road to peace than the one that starts from little islands and oases of genuine kind-

ness, islands and oases constantly growing in number and being continually joined together until eventually they ring the world."
—*FATHER DOMINIQUE PIRE* (1958)

"The sacred union existing between two brother human beings who rediscover themselves as men of true dignity while working together to save a third rids us of many of the barriers of prejudice, narrow-mindedness, and discrimination that poison human love and sap its strength. We must now have faith in the power of love and set it to work. Let me point out right away that a gesture of brotherly love extended jointly requires no compromise of principle, but on the contrary is justified and indeed welcomed by the right-minded. Let us not speak of *tolerance*. This negative word implies grudging concessions by smug consciences. Rather, let us speak of mutual understanding and mutual respect."
—*FATHER DOMINIQUE PIRE* (1958)

"In a strife-torn world, tottering on the brink of complete destruction by man-made nuclear weapons, a free and independent Africa is in the making, in answer to the injunction and challenge of history: 'Arise and shine for thy light is come.' Acting in concert with other nations, she is man's last hope for a mediator between the East and West, and is qualified to demand of the great powers to 'turn the swords into ploughshares' because two-thirds of mankind is hungry and illiterate; to engage human energy, human skill, and human talent in the service of peace, for the alternative is unthinkable—war, destruction, and desolation; and to build a world community which will stand as a lasting monument to the millions of men and women, to such devoted and distinguished world citizens and fighters for peace as the late Dag Hammarskjöld, who have given their lives that we may live in happiness and peace.

"Africa's qualification for this noble task is incontestable, for her own fight has never been and is not now a fight for conquest of land, for accumulation of wealth or domination of peoples, but for the recognition and preservation of the rights of man and the establishment of a truly free world for a free people."

—*ALBERT JOHN LUTULI* (1960)

"Is the Red Cross in wartime a flickering flame to remind us of our continuing brotherhood? Is it a gesture to declare, despite appearances, that we are derived from the Godhead; that we may lay waste our bodies but cannot cast aside, entirely, our souls?

"It is this contrast between the work of the Red Cross in peace and in war that provides an endless fascination. In peace, it is the strong support of beneficent service, and in emergencies a wave and pillar of succor for the distressed. In war, it is a liaison, a medium of practical help to the wounded and the prisoner, a symbol that beyond the knives and guns, the larks and the angels are watching."

—*JOHN A. MACAULAY*, representing
the League of Red Cross Societies *(1963)*

Albert John Lutuli, former Zulu tribal chief and leader against apartheid policies in South Africa (1960).

"A famous poet once inquired: 'Where are the snows of yesteryear?' Perhaps we shall live to the day when men will ask: 'Where are the hates of yesteryear?' For, in the long run, the power of kindness can redeem beyond the power of force to destroy. There is a vast reservoir of kindness that we can no longer afford to disregard.

"The curtain is lifting. We can have Triumph or Tragedy—for we are the playwrights, the actors, and the audience. Let us book our seats for Triumph—the world is sickened of Tragedy."

—*JOHN A. MACAULAY,* representing
the League of Red Cross Societies   *(1963)*

"Today I come to Oslo as a trustee, inspired and with renewed dedication to humanity. I accept this prize on behalf of all men who love peace and brotherhood. I say I come as a trustee, for in the depths of my heart I am aware that this prize is much more than an honor to me personally.

"Every time I take a flight, I am always mindful of the many people who make a successful journey possible— the known pilots and the unknown ground crew. You honor the dedicated pilots of our struggle who have sat at the controls as the freedom movement soared into orbit. You honor, once again, Chief Lutuli of South Africa, whose struggles with and for his people, are still met with the most brutal expression of man's inhumanity to man. You honor the ground crew without whose labor and sacrifice the jet flights to freedom could never have left the earth. Most of these people will never make the headlines and their names will not appear in *Who's Who*. Yet when years have rolled past and when the blazing light of truth is focused on this marvelous age in which we live—men and women will know and children will be taught that we have a finer land, a better people, a more noble civilization—because these humble children of god were willing to suffer for righteousness' sake.

"I think Alfred Nobel would know what I mean when I say that I accept this award in the spirit of a curator of some precious heirloom which he holds in trust for its true owners—all those to whom beauty is truth and truth beauty—and in whose eyes the beauty of genuine brotherhood and peace is more precious than diamonds or silver or gold."

—*MARTIN LUTHER KING, JR.* *(1964)*

"The voice of women has a special role and a special soul-force in the struggle for a nonviolent world. We do not wish to replace religious sectarianism or ideological division with sexism or any kind of militant feminism. But we do believe that women have a leading role to play in this great struggle.

"So we are honored, in the name of all women, that women have been honored especially for their part in leading a nonviolent movement for a just and peaceful society. Compassion is more important than intellect in

calling forth the love that the work of peace needs, and
intuition can often be a far more powerful searchlight
than cold reason. We have to think, and think hard, but
if we do not have compassion before we even start
thinking, then we are quite likely to start fighting over
theories. . . .

"Because of the role of women over so many centuries in so many different cultures, they have been ex-
cluded from what have been called public affairs; for that
very reason they have concentrated much more on
things close to home . . . and they have kept far more in
touch with the true realities . . . the realities of giving
birth and love. The moment has perhaps come in human
history when, for very surivial, those realities must be
given pride of place over the vainglorious adventures
that lead to war.

"But we do not wish to see a division over this . . .
merely a natural and respectful and loving cooperation.
Women and men together can make this a beautiful people's world, and that is why we called ourselves 'THE
PEACE PEOPLE.' "

—BETTY WILLIAMS (1976)

"At times our members have gained more from the
prisoner they sought to help than the prisoner has
gained from them: much of courage, of the value of
human dignity and freedom, of the durability of the
human spirit.

"It is for this reason that our last word should belong
to a prisoner.

"Some time ago, one of them, now dead, was able to send a letter from prison in which she wrote:

They are envious of us. They will envy us all, for it is an enviable but very difficult task to live through a history as a human being, to complete a life as a human being. Soon the night will fall and they will close the doors of the cell. I feel lonely. No . . . I am with the whole of mankind and the whole of mankind is with me.

—*MÜMTAZ SOYSAL,* representing
Amnesty International *(1977)*

"From this platform of peace, I would like to appeal to all those in whose hands the future of mankind lies, to use their power not to destroy or kill, not to create suffering in a grasping search for selfish objectives, but to help alleviate the plight of the needy; to aim at justice and freedom for the individual.

"And I appeal to each and every one. Let us never cease to feel compassion for those in want. Let us never tire of helping victims of injustice and oppression. He who puts his faith in the restoration of human dignity cannot be wrong."

—*POUL HARTLING,* representing the
Office of the United Nations High
Commissioner for Refugees *(1981)*

"I come from a beautiful land, richly endowed by God with wonderful natural resources, wide expanses, rolling mountains, singing birds, bright shining stars out of blue skies, with radiant sunshine, golden sunshine. There is enough of the good things that come from God's bounty, there is enough for everyone, but apartheid has confirmed some in their selfishness, causing them to grasp greedily a disproportionate share, the lion's share, because of their power."

—DESMOND MPILO TUTU (1984)

"There is no peace in Southern Africa. There is no peace because there is no justice. There can be no real peace and security until there be first justice enjoyed by all the inhabitants of that beautiful land. The Bible knows nothing about peace without justice, for that would be crying, 'Peace, peace, where there is no peace.' God's Shalom, peace, involves inevitably righteousness, justice, wholeness, fullness of life, participation in decision making, goodness, laughter, joy, compassion, sharing, and reconciliation."

—DESMOND MPILO TUTU (1984)

"Because there is global insecurity, nations are engaged in a mad arms race, spending billions of dollars wastefully on instruments of destruction, when millions are starving. And yet, just a fraction of what is expended

43

so obscenely on defense budgets would make the difference in enabling God's children to fill their stomachs, be educated, and be given the chance to lead fulfilled and happy lives. We have the capacity to feed ourselves several times over, but we are daily haunted by the spectacle of the gaunt dregs of humanity shuffling along in endless queues, with bowls to collect what the charity of the world has provided, too little too late. When will we learn, when will the people of the world get up and say, Enough is enough. God created us for fellowship. God created us so that we should form the human family, existing together because we were made for one another. We are not made for an exclusive self-sufficiency but for interdependence, and we break the law of our being at our peril."

—*DESMOND MPILO TUTU* (1984)

"The problems we face today, violent conflicts, destruction of nature, poverty, hunger, and so on, are human-created problems which can be resolved through human effort, understanding and the development of a sense of brotherhood and sisterhood. We need to cultivate a universal responsibility for one another and the planet we share. Although I have found my own Buddhist religion helpful in generating love and compassion, even for those we consider our enemies, I am convinced that everyone can develop a good heart and a sense of universal responsibility with or without religion."

—*THE DALAI LAMA* (1989)

Mother Teresa, founder of the Roman Catholic order Missionaries of Charity in Calcutta, hugging a child on a visit to New York (1981).

FAITH
AND
HOPE

"Consider the way that poets, with few exceptions, pay court to fame and popularity by singing the praises of war and massacre. Consider again how the most sublime virtues are always associated with the national flag while cruelty is ascribed to the enemy alone—this in order to sustain mistrust, hatred, and enmity between nations. Remembering and pondering all this, oh, I confess to you that I too have had moments of discouragement, wondering whether the idea to which I devote, and have for years devoted, all my time and energy might be no more than an illusion of my poor mind, a dream like Thomas More's *Utopia* or our own Campanella's *City of the Sun*.

"But these were fleeting moments! And I was soon telling myself that if work for a future of peace and justice, a future of continual progress and of fruitful and useful labor for all men and all nations, was indeed an illusion, it was still an illusion so divine as to make life worth living and to inspire one to die for it.

"But it is not an illusion. I felt this deep within me, and the history of human evolution as well as everyday experience confirmed it for me. Reasonable ideas which find their sanction in the conscience of the righteous do not die; they are consequently realities and active forces, but they are so only to the extent that those who profess them know how to turn them to account. It depends on us, then, and on our judgment and steadfastness whether or not the idea of peace will root itself ever more firmly in public awareness until it grows into the living and active conscience of a whole people."

— *ERNESTO TEODORO MONETA* (1907)

49

Léon Bourgeois, French political leader, who was appointed the first president of the League of Nations in 1920.

"To climb by all roads originating from all points of the world to the pinnacle where the law of man itself holds sway in sovereign rhythm—is this not the ultimate end of mankind's painful and centuries-long ascent of calvary?

"To be sure, many years of trial must yet elapse, and many retrogressions yet occur, before the rumble of human passions common to all men yields to silence; but if the road toward the final goal is clearly marked, if an organization like the League of Nations realizes its potential and achieves its purpose, the potent benefits of peace and of human solidarity will triumph over evil. This at least we may dare to hope for; and, if we will consider how far we have come since the dawn of history, then our hope will gather strength enough to become a true and unshakable faith."

—LÉON BOURGEOIS (1920)

"Therefore, all hope of a better future for mankind rests on the promotion of 'a higher form of development for world civilization,' an all-embracing human community. Are we right in adopting a teleological viewpoint, a belief that a radiant and beneficent purpose guides the fate of men and of nations and will lead us forward to that higher stage of social development? In propaganda work we must necessarily build upon such an optimistic assumption. Propaganda must appeal to mankind's better judgment and to the necessary belief in a better future. For this belief, the valley of the shadow of death is but a way station on the road to the blessed summit."

—CHRISTIAN L. LANGE (1921)

"There are surely many of us who can only regard the belief in personal immortality as a claim which must remain unproved—a projection of the eternity concept onto the personal level.

"Should we then be compelled to believe that the theory of materialism expressed in the old Arab parable of the bush whose leaves fall withered to the ground and die without leaving a trace behind truly applies to the family of man?

"It seems to me that the theory of mankind's organic unity and eternal continuity raises the materialistic view to a higher level.

"The idea of eternity lives in all of us. We thirst to live in a belief which raises our small personality to a higher coherence—a coherence which is human and yet superhuman, absolute and yet steadily growing and developing, ideal and yet real.

"Can this desire ever be fulfilled? It seems to be a contradiction in terms.

"And yet there is a belief which satisfies this desire and resolves the contradiction.

"It is the belief in the unity of mankind."
                              —*CHRISTIAN L. LANGE* (1921)

"If peace is to become a reality on our earth, it must be founded in the hearts of the people. To whom should this task belong if not to the church, which calls itself the Prince of Peace and has as its watchword what is also a divine promise: Glory to God in the highest and peace on earth. The human heart is fickle, and therefore peace

must, according to the words of the prophets, be safe-
guarded by law and order, by a supranational judicial
system which has the power to assert itself against nations endangering peace and which, without bias or
compromise, holds justice to be the highest law. Never-
theless, any such legal system, however wise and strong,
remains a mere shell if not supported by mankind's concern for peace and liberty. . . . But if a body does not
possess a soul, it differs little from a machine. In this in-
stance, the soul is the love and justice of the Gospel, not
the demon of selfishness."

—*NATHAN SÖDERBLOM* *(1930)*

"We do not believe with Socrates that man does what
is right because he knows it to be right, but we must
agree with the philosopher in that man needs to know
what is right before he acts."

—*NATHAN SÖDERBLOM* *(1930)*

"We must not stumble over the barriers we meet. We
must run hard, for sometimes we must leap high to sur-
mount the difficulties of fulfilling our obligations to humanity. We must not let ourselves be torn by the thorns
of thickets obstructing the 'savage paths' of which I
spoke earlier. We must look higher and at the same time
nearer. We must draw close in body and in spirit in

order to merit the name by which the magnificent symbol of the Red Cross calls us, the name Man, the name
Christian."

—ÉDOUARD CHAPUISAT, representing
the International Committee of the Red
Cross *(1944)*

"I have spoken against fear as a basis for peace. What
we ought to fear, especially we Americans, is not that
someone may drop atomic bombs on us but that we may
allow a world situation to develop in which ordinarily
reasonable and humane men, acting as our representa-
tives, may use such weapons in our name. We ought to
be resolved beforehand that no provocation, no tempta-
tion shall induce us to resort to the last dreadful alternative of war.

"May no young man ever again be faced with the
choice between violating his conscience by cooperating
in competitive mass slaughter or separating himself from
those who, endeavoring to serve liberty, democracy, humanity, can find no better way than to conscript young
men to kill.

"As the world community develops in peace, it will
open up great untapped reservoirs in human nature. Like
a spring released from pressure would be the response
of a generation of young men and women growing up in
an atmosphere of friendliness and security, in a world
demanding their service, offering them comradeship,
calling to all adventurous and forward-reaching natures.

"We are not asked to subscribe to any utopia or to believe in a perfect world just around the corner. We are asked to be patient with necessarily slow and groping advance on the road forward, and to be ready for each step ahead as it becomes practicable. We are asked to equip ourselves with courage, hope, readiness for hard work, and to cherish large and generous ideals."

—*EMILY GREENE BALCH* *(1946)*

"This international service is not mere humanitarianism; it is not merely mopping up, cleaning up the world after war. It is aimed at creating peace by setting an example of a different way of international service. So our foreign relief is a means of rehabilitation and it is intended not merely to help the body but to help the spirit and to give men hope that there can be a peaceful world."

—*HENRY CADBURY*, representing the American Friends Service Committee *(1947)*   ·

"Upon this basic truth all the principles and actions of the Society of Friends are founded. Each man is seen as having intrinsic value, and Christ is equally concerned for the other man as for me. We all become part of the divine family, and as such we are all responsible for one another, carrying our share of the shame when wrong is done and of the burden of suffering."

—*MARGARET BACKHOUSE,*
representing the Friends
Service Council of Great
Britain *(1947)*

"For Europe at least, peace is inevitable. It can be either the peace of the grave, the peace of the dead empires of the past, which lost their creative spirit and failed to adjust themselves to new conditions, or a new dynamic peace applying science in a great leap forward in the evolution of human society to a new age in which hunger, poverty, and preventible diseases will be eliminated from the earth—an age in which the people in every country will rise to a far higher level of intellectual and cultural well-being, an age in which 'iron curtains' will disappear and people, though intensely patriotic for their own country, will be able to travel freely as world citizens. That is the hope science sets before us."

—*JOHN BOYD-ORR (1949)*

"I am not an old admiral receiving the last and most magnificent decoration of his life. It is a profound joy, a joy of the soul, like that of a mountaineer who, half way up, has just had a sudden glimpse of the path which will allow him to climb farther and better."

—*FATHER DOMINIQUE PIRE (1958)*

"Now we are forced to eliminate from the world forever this vestige of prehistoric barbarism, this curse to
the human race. We, you and I, are privileged to be
alive during this extraordinary age, this unique epoch in
the history of the world, the epoch of demarcation between the past millennia of war and suffering, and the
future, the great future of peace, justice, morality, and
human well-being. We are privileged to have the opportunity of contributing to the achievement of the goal of
the abolition of war and its replacement by world law. I
am confident that we shall succeed in this great task; that
the world community will thereby be freed not only
from the suffering caused by war but also, through the
better use of the earth's resources, of the discoveries of
scientists, and of the efforts of mankind, from hunger,
disease, illiteracy, and fear; and that we shall in the
course of time be enabled to build a world characterized
by economic, political, and social justice for all human
beings and a culture worthy of man's intelligence."

—*LINUS PAULING* *(1962)*

"I accept this award today with an abiding faith in
America and an audacious faith in the future of mankind. I refuse to accept despair as the final response to
the ambiguities of history. I refuse to accept the idea
that the 'isness' of man's present nature makes him mor-
ally incapable of reaching up for the eternal 'oughtness'
that forever confronts him. I refuse to accept the idea

that man is mere flotsam and jetsam in the river of
life unable to influence the unfolding events which sur-
round him."
—*MARTIN LUTHER KING, JR.* *(1964)*

"So we must fix our vision not merely on the negative
expulsion of war, but upon the positive affirmation of
peace. We must see that peace represents a sweet music,
a cosmic melody that is far superior to the discords of
war. Somehow we must transform the dynamics of the
world power struggle from the negative nuclear arms
race which no one can win to a positive contest to har-
ness man's creative genius for the purpose of making
peace and prosperity a reality for all of the nations of
the world. In short, we must shift the arms race into a
'peace race.' If we have the will and determination to
mount such a peace offensive, we will unlock hitherto
tightly sealed doors of hope and transform our imminent
cosmic elegy into a psalm of creative fulfillment."
—*MARTIN LUTHER KING, JR.* *(1964)*

"In my view the role of voluntary organizations is becoming more and more essential. They are the only bodies that will have the necessary independence and
initiative to restore some faith and idealism in our world.
They deserve a great deal more support and encourage-
ment.

"If disarmament can be achieved it will be due to the untiring, selfless work of the non-governmental sector. This is what Alfred Nobel appreciated in his days. It is more urgent than ever now. The big powers are traveling on the dangerous road of armament. The signpost just ahead of us is 'Oblivion.' Can the march on this road be stopped? Yes, if public opinion uses the power it now has."

—*SEAN MACBRIDE   (1974)*

"Other civilizations, including more 'successful' ones, should exist an infinite number of times on the 'preceding' and the 'following' pages of the Book of the Universe. Yet this should not minimize our sacred endeavors in this world of ours, where, like faint glimmers of light in the dark, we have emerged for a moment from the nothingness of dark unconsciousness of material existence. We must make good the demands of reason and create a life worthy of ourselves and of the goals we only dimly perceive."

—*ANDREI SAKHAROV   (1975)*

"The poor are very wonderful people. One evening we went out and we picked up four people from the street. And one of them was in a most terrible condition—and I told the sisters: You take care of the other three, I take care of this one who looked worse. So I did for her all that my love can do. I put her in bed, and there was such a beautiful smile on her face. She took hold of my hand as she said just the words 'Thank you,' and she died.

"I could not help but examine my conscience before her, and I asked what would I say if I was in her place. And my answer was very simple. I would have tried to draw a little attention to myself, I would have said I am hungry, that I am dying, I am cold, I am in pain, or something, but she gave me much more—she gave me her grateful love. And she died with a smile on her face. As did that man whom we picked up from the drain, half eaten with worms, and we brought him to the home. 'I have lived like an animal in the street, but I am going to die like an angel, loved and cared for.' And it was so wonderful to see the greatness of that man who could speak like that, who could die like that without blaming anybody, without cursing anybody, without comparing anything. Like an angel—this is the greatness of our people. And that is why we believe what Jesus had said: I was hungry—I was naked—I was homeless—I was unwanted, unloved, uncared for—and you did it to me.

"I believe that we are not real social workers. We may be doing social work in the eyes of the people, but we are really contemplatives in the heart of the world. For we are touching the body of Christ twenty-four hours. . . . And I think that in our family we don't need bombs and guns, to destroy, to bring peace—just get together, love one another, bring that peace, that joy, that strength of presence of each other in the home. And we will be able to overcome all the evil that is in the world."

—*MOTHER TERESA* *(1979)*

"And with this prize that I have received as a Prize of Peace, I am going to try to make the home for many people who have no home. Because I believe that love begins at home, and if we can create a home for the poor I think that more and more love will spread. And we will be able through this understanding love to bring peace, be the good news to the poor. The poor in our own family first, in our country and in the world. To be able to do this, our Sisters, our lives have to be woven with prayer. They have to be woven with Christ to be able to understand, to be able to share. Because to be woven with Christ is to be able to understand, to be able to share. Because today there is so much suffering. . . . When I pick up a person from the street, hungry, I give him a plate of rice, a piece of bread, I have satisfied. I have removed that hunger. But a person who is shut out, who feels unwanted, unloved, terrified, the person who has been thrown out from society—that poverty is so full of hurt and so unbearable, and I find that very difficult. . . . And so let us always meet each other with a smile, for the smile is the beginning of love, and once we begin to love each other naturally we want to do something."

—*MOTHER TERESA* *(1979)*

"We live in hope because we believe, like St. Paul, that love never dies. Human beings in the historical process have created enclaves of love by their active practice of solidarity throughout the world, and with a view to the full-orbed liberation of peoples and all humanity.

"For me it is essential to have the inward peace and serenity of prayer in order to listen to the silence of God, which speaks to us, in our personal lives and in the history of our times, about the power of love.

"Because of our faith in Christ and humankind, we must apply our humble efforts to the construction of a more just and humane world. And I want to declare emphatically: *Such a world is possible.*

"To create this new society, we must present outstretched and friendly hands, without hatred and rancor, even as we show great determination and never waver in the defense of truth and justice. Because we know that we cannot sow seeds with clenched fists. To sow we must open our hands."

—*ADOLFO PÉREZ ESQUIVEL (1980)*

"My voice would like to have the strength of the voice of the humble and lowly. It is a voice that denounces injustice and proclaims hope in God and humanity. For this hope is the hope of all human beings who yearn to live in communion with all persons as their brothers and sisters and as children of God."

—*ADOLFO PÉREZ ESQUIVEL (1980)*

"The prize has given fresh hope to many in a world
that has sometimes had a pall of despondency cast over
it by the experience of suffering, disease, poverty, fam-
ine, hunger, oppression, injustice, evil, and war. A pall
that has made many wonder whether God cares, whether
he was omnipotent, whether he was loving and compas-
sionate."

—*DESMOND MPILO TUTU (1984)*

"New hope has sprung in the breast of many as a re-
sult of this prize: a mother watching her child starve in
front of some homeland resettlement camp, or one
whose flimsy plastic shelter was demolished by the au-
thorities in the KTC squatters' camp in Cape Town; the
man emasculated, who lived for eleven months in single-
sex hostels; the student receiving an inferior education;
the activist languishing in a consulate or a solitary con-
finement cell, being tortured because he thought he was
human and wanted that God-given right recognized; the
exile longing to kiss the soil of her much-loved motherland; the political prisoner watching the days of a life
sentence go by like the drip of a faulty tap, imprisoned
because he knew he was created by God not to have his
human dignity and pride trodden underfoot. A new
hope has been kindled in the breasts of the millions who
are voiceless, oppressed, dispossessed, tortured by the
powerful tyrants, lacking elementary human rights in
Latin America, Southeast Asia, in the Far East, many
parts of Africa, and behind the Iron Curtain, who have
their noses rubbed in the dust.

Archbishop Desmond Tutu preaching in Hartford, Connecticut, on his tour of the United States (1986).

"How wonderful, how appropriate that this award is made today, December 10, Human Rights Day. It says more eloquently than anything else that this is God's world, and He is in charge; that our cause is a just cause; that we will obtain human rights across Africa and everywhere in the world; we shall be free in South Africa and everywhere in the world. . . .

"On behalf of all these for whom you have given new hope, a new cause for joy, I want to accept this award in a wholly representative capacity.

"I accept this prestigious award on behalf of my family, on behalf of the South African Council of Churches, on behalf of all in my motherland, on behalf of those committed to the cause of justice, peace, and reconciliation everywhere.

"If God be for us who can be against us?"

—*DESMOND MPILO TUTU* (1984)

"For the physician, whose role is to affirm life, optimism is a medical imperative. Even when the outcome is doubtful, a patient's hopeful attitude promotes well-being and frequently leads to recovery. Pessimism degrades the quality of life and jeopardizes the tomorrows yet to come. An affirmative world view is essential if we are to shape a more promising future.

"The American poet Langston Hughes urged:

Hold on to dreams
For if dreams die,
Life is a broken winged bird
And cannot fly.

"We must hold fast to the dream that reason will prevail. The world today is full of anguish and dread. As great as is the danger, still greater is the opportunity. If science and technology have catapulted us to the brink of extinction, the same ingenuity has brought humankind to the boundary of an age of abundance.

"Never before was it possible to feed all the hungry. Never before was it possible to shelter all the homeless. Never before was it possible to teach all the illiterates. Never before were we able to heal so many afflictions. For the first time science and medicine can diminish drudgery and pain.

"Only those who can see the invisible can do the impossible. But in order to do the impossible, in the words of Jonathan Schell, we ask 'not for our personal survival: we ask only that we be survived. We ask for assurance that when we die as individuals, as we know we must, mankind will live on.'

"If we are to succeed, this vision must possess millions of people. We must convince each generation that they are but transient passengers on this planet earth. It does not belong to them. They are not free to doom generations yet unborn. They are not at liberty to erase humanity's past nor dim its future. Only life itself can lay claim to sacred continuity. The magnitude of the danger and its imminence must bring the human family together in a common pursuit of peace denied throughout this century. On the threshold of a new millennium the achievement of world peace is no longer remote, for it is beckoned by the unleashing of the deepest spiritual forces embedded in humankind when threatened with extinction. The reason, the creativeness, and the courage

that human beings possess foster an abiding faith that
what humanity creates, humanity can and will control."
—*DR. EVGENY CHAZOV,* representing
International Physicians for the
Prevention of Nuclear War *(1985)*

"Hope is the strongest driving force for a people.
Hope which brings about change, which produces new
realities, is what opens man's road to freedom. Once
hope has taken hold, courage must unite with wisdom.
That is the only way of avoiding violence, the only way
of maintaining the calm one needs to respond peacefully
to offenses."
—*OSCAR ARIAS SÁNCHEZ (1987)*

"History was not written by men who predicted failure, who gave up their dreams, who abandoned their
principles, who allowed their laziness to put their intelligence to sleep."
—*OSCAR ARIAS SÁNCHEZ (1987)*

"Seeing the size of the challenge, no wonder many are prey to discouragement; or that apocalyptic prophets abound, announcing the failures of the fight against poverty, proclaiming the immediate fall of the democracies, forecasting the futility of peacemaking efforts.

"I do not share this defeatism. I cannot accept that to be realistic means to tolerate misery, violence, and hate. I do not believe that the hungry man should be treated as subversive for expressing his suffering. I shall never accept that the law can be used to justify tragedy, to keep things as they are, to make us abandon our ideas of a different world. Law is the path of liberty, and must as such open the way to progress for everyone."

—*OSCAR ARIAS SÁNCHEZ* *(1987)*

"I feel honored, humbled and deeply moved that you should give this important prize to a simple monk from Tibet. I am no one special. But I believe the prize is a recognition of the true value of altruism, love, compassion and nonviolence which I try to practice, in accordance with the teachings of the Buddha and the great sages of India and Tibet."

—*THE DALAI LAMA* *(1989)*

"As a Buddhist monk, my concern extends to all members of the human family and, indeed, to all sentient beings who suffer. I believe all suffering is caused by ignorance. People inflict pain on others in the selfish pursuit of their happiness or satisfaction. Yet true happiness comes from a sense of inner peace and contentment, which in turn must be achieved through the cultivation of altruism, of love and compassion, and elimination of ignorance, selfishness and greed."

—*THE DALAI LAMA (1989)*

"I believe all religions pursue the same goals, that of cultivating human goodness and bringing happiness to all human beings. Though the means might appear different, the ends are the same. As we enter the final decade of this century I am optimistic that the ancient values that have sustained mankind are today reaffirming themselves to prepare us for a kinder, happier twenty-first century."

—*THE DALAI LAMA (1989)*

"It is my dream that the entire Tibetan plateau should become a free refuge where humanity and nature can live in peace and in harmonious balance. It would be a place where people from all over the world could come to seek the true meaning of peace within themselves, away from the tensions and pressures of much of the rest of the world. Tibet could indeed become a creative center for the promotion and development of peace."

—*THE DALAI LAMA (1989)*

Elie Wiesel praying at the Unknown Jewish Martyr's Memorial in Paris (1987).

THE
TRAGEDY
OF
WAR

"One day . . . I watched, from the windows of my home, three Austrian soldiers fall amid a hail of bullets. Apparently dead, they were carried away to a neighboring square. I saw them again two hours later: one of them was still in the throes of dying. This sight froze the blood in my veins and I was overcome by a great compassion. In these three soldiers I no longer saw enemies, but men like myself, and with remorse as keenly suffered as if I had killed them with my own hands, I thought of their families, who were perhaps at that very moment preparing for their return.

"In that instant I felt all the cruelty and inhumanity of war which sets peoples against one another to their mutual detriment, peoples who should have every interest in understanding and being friends with each other. I was to feel this way many times as I looked at the dead and the wounded in all the wars for our independence in which I took part."

—*ERNESTO TEODORO MONETA* *(1907)*

"In the Capitoline Museum in Rome is a sculpture in marble which, in its simple pathos, seems to me to be a most beautiful creation. It is the statue of the 'Dying Gaul.' He is lying on the battlefield, mortally wounded. The vigorous body, hardened by work and combat, is sinking into death. The head, with its coarse hair, is bowed, the strong neck bends, the rough powerful workman's hand, till recently wielding the sword, now presses against the ground in a last effort to hold up the drooping body.

"He was driven to fight for foreign gods whom he did not know, far from his country. And thus he met his fate. Now he lies there, dying in silence. The noise of the fray no longer reaches his ear. His dimmed eyes are turned inward, perhaps on a final vision of his childhood home, where life was simple and happy, of his birthplace deep in the forest of Gaul.

"That is how I see mankind in its suffering; that is how I see the suffering people of Europe, bleeding to death on deserted battlefields after conflicts which to a great extent were not their own.

"This is the outcome of the lust for power, the imperialism, the militarism, that have run amok across the earth."

—FRIDTJOF NANSEN (1922)

"Let us face squarely the paradox that the world which goes to war is a world, usually, genuinely desiring peace. War is the outcome, not mainly of evil intentions, but on the whole, of good intentions which miscarry or are frustrated. It is made, not usually by evil men knowing themselves to be wrong, but is the outcome of policies pursued by good men usually passionately convinced that they are right."

—NORMAN ANGELL (1933)

"Who, indeed, could be so unseeing as not to realize that in modern war victory is illusory; that the harvest of war can be only misery, destruction, and degradation?

"If war should come, the peoples of the world would again be called upon to fight it, but they would not have willed it.

"Statesmen and philosophers repeatedly have warned that some values—freedom, honor, self-respect—are higher than peace or life itself. This may be true. Certainly, very many would hold that the loss of human dignity and self-respect, the chains of enslavement, are too high a price even for peace. But the horrible realities of modern warfare scarcely afford even this fatal choice. There is only suicidal escape, not freedom, in the death and destruction of atomic war. This is mankind's great dilemma. The well-being and the hopes of the peoples of the world can never be served until peace—as well as freedom, honor and self-respect—is secure."

—*RALPH J. BUNCHE* (1950)

"Throughout the ages . . . man has but little heeded the advice of the wise men. He has been—fatefully, if not willfully—less virtuous, less constant, less rational, less peaceful than he knows how to be, than he is fully capable of being. He has been led astray from the ways of peace and brotherhood by his addiction to concepts and attitudes of narrow nationalism, racial and religious bigotry, greed and lust for power. Despite this, despite the almost continuous state of war to which bad human relations have condemned him, he has made steady progress. In his scientific genius, man has wrought material miracles and has transformed his world. He has harnessed nature and has developed great civilizations. But he has never learned very well how to live with himself. The values he has created have been predominantly materialistic; his spiritual values have lagged far behind. He has demonstrated little spiritual genius and has made little progress toward the realization of human brotherhood. In the contemporary atomic age, this could prove man's fatal weakness.

"Alfred Nobel, a half-century ago, foresaw with prophetic vision that if the complacent mankind of his day could, with equanimity, contemplate war, the day would soon inevitably come when man would be confronted with the fateful alternative of peace or reversion to the Dark Ages. Man may well ponder whether he has not now reached that stage. Man's inventive genius has so far outstretched his reason—not his capacity to reason but his willingness to apply reason—that the peoples of the world find themselves precariously on the brink of total disaster."

—*RALPH J. BUNCHE* (1950)

"But the essential fact which we should acknowledge in our conscience, and which we should have acknowledged a long time ago, is that we are becoming inhuman to the extent that we become supermen. We have learned to tolerate the facts of war: that men are killed en masse—some twenty million in the Second World War—that whole cities and their inhabitants are annihilated by the atomic bomb, that men are turned into living torches by incendiary bombs. We learn of these things from the radio or newspapers and we judge them according to whether they signify success for the group of peoples to which we belong, or for our enemies. When we do admit to ourselves that such acts are the results of inhuman conduct, our admission is accompanied by the thought that the very fact of war itself leaves us no option but to accept them. In resigning ourselves to our fate without a struggle, we are guilty of inhumanity.

"What really matters is that we should all of us realize that we are guilty of inhumanity. The horror of this realization should shake us out of our lethargy so that we can direct our hopes and our intentions to the coming of an era in which war will have no place. This hope and this will can have but one aim: to attain, through a change in spirit, that superior reason which will dissuade us from misusing the power at our disposal."

—*ALBERT SCHWEITZER* (1952)

"There has been considerable comment over the awarding of the Nobel Peace Prize to a soldier. I am afraid this does not seem as remarkable to me as it quite evidently appears to others. I know a great deal of the horrors and tragedies of war. Today, as chairman of the American Battle Monuments Commission, it is my duty to supervise the construction and maintenance of military cemeteries in many countries overseas. . . . The cost of war in human lives is constantly spread before me,

written neatly in many ledgers whose columns are grave-
stones. I am deeply moved to find some means or
method of avoiding another calamity of war."
                    —*GEORGE C. MARSHALL* (1953)

"Today, less than ever, can we defend ourselves by
force, for there is no effective defense against the all-
destroying effect of nuclear missile weapons. Indeed,
their very power has made their use intolerable, even
unthinkable, because of the annihilative retaliation in
kind that such use would invoke. So peace remains, as
the phrase goes, balanced uneasily on terror, and the use
of maximum force is frustrated by the certainty that it
will be used in reply with a totally devastating effect.
Peace, however, must surely be more than this trembling
rejection of universal suicide.

"The stark and inescapable fact is that today we cannot
defend our society by war since total war is total destruction, and if war is used as an instrument of policy,
eventually we will have total war. Therefore, the best
defense of peace is not power, but the removal of the
causes of war, and international agreements which will
put peace on a stronger foundation than the terror of
destruction."
                    —*LESTER B. PEARSON* (1957)

"No dispute between nations can justify nuclear war.
There is no defense against nuclear weapons that could

not be overcome by increasing the scale of the attack. It would be contrary to the nature of war for nations to adhere to agreements to fight 'limited' wars, using only 'small' nuclear weapons—even little wars today are perilous, because of the likelihood that a little war would grow into a world catastrophe."

—*LINUS PAULING* *(1962)*

"I am intentionally not using the phrase 'striving for peace' too frequently. The longing for peace is rooted in the hearts of all men. But the striving, which at present has become so insistent, cannot lay claim to leading the way to eternal peace, or solving all disputes among nations, so strong are the economic and political roots. Nor can it create a lasting state of harmonious understanding between men. Our immediate striving must be aimed at preventing what, in the present situation, is the greatest threat to the very survival of mankind, the nuclear threat."

—*ALVA REIMER MYRDAL* *(1982)*

"The world, generally speaking, is now drifting on a more and more devastating course towards one single and absurd target of extermination—or rather, to be more exact—the northern hemisphere's towns, fields, and the people who have developed our civilization.

"The distressing situation of our age, which recalls the

Alva Myrdal, Swedish social reformer and disarmament negotiator (1969).

fate that overtook Rome, conceals—together with political and economic factors—a clearly irredeemable misconception, viz. that the use of weapons of war, *violence,*
can lead to *victory.*

"Would it be possible, at immense expense, to inaugu-
rate a new and happy existence for the world on the
ruins of one that would be at least half-destroyed? The
misconception that 'a victory is worth the price' has in
the nuclear age become a total illusion."

—*ALVA REIMER MYRDAL* *(1982)*

"The experts have as a rule arrived at the conclusion
that the target for a sufficient deterrent would involve
something like 400 missiles, capable of reaching from
one continent to the other. Any developments over and
above this have simply meant one more step in the direction of increased instability. It has been unnecessary,
and at what a cost! . . .

"I shall go on repeating, until the politicians get it into
their heads, that 'when one has enough, one does not
need more.' "

—*ALVA REIMER MYRDAL* *(1982)*

"I am convinced that today is a great and exciting day
not only for the members of our international movement
but also for all physicians on our planet, irrespective of
their political and religious beliefs. For the first time in

81

history, their selfless service for the cause of maintaining life on earth is marked by the high Nobel Prize. True to the Hippocratic Oath, we cannot keep silent knowing what the final epidemic—nuclear war—can bring to humankind. The bell of Hiroshima rings in our hearts not as a funeral knell but as an alarm bell calling out to actions to protect life on our planet."

> —*DR. EVGENY CHAZOV*, representing
> International Physicians for the
> Prevention of Nuclear War   *(1985)*

"In our medical practice when we deal with a critical patient, in order to save him we mobilize all our energies and knowledge, sacrifice part of our hearts, enlist the cooperation of our most experienced colleagues. Today we face seriously ill humanity torn apart by distrust and fear of nuclear war. To save it we must arouse the conscience of the world's peoples, cultivate hate for nuclear weapons, repudiate egoism and chauvinism, create a favorable atmosphere of trust. In the nuclear age we are all interdependent. The earth is our only common home, which we cannot abandon. The new suicidal situation calls for the new thinking. We must convince those who make political decisions of this.

"Our professional duty is to protect life on earth. True to the Hippocratic Oath, physicians will dedicate their knowledge, their hearts and their lives to the happiness of their patients and well-being of the peoples of the world."

> —*DR. EVGENY CHAZOV*, representing
> International Physicians for the
> Prevention of Nuclear War   *(1985)*

"We Soviet physicians, who know what a devastating
war is like, not from history textbooks but from our own
experience, who, together with all our people filled with
hatred for war—we were troubled by the indifference
demonstrated by many towards these irresponsible state-
ments justifying the nuclear arms race. It was necessary
to arouse the indifferent and turn them into active opponents of nuclear weapons. It was not simply our obligation as honest men, it was our professional duty. As
Hippocrates said: 'The physician must inform the patient
about everything that threatens his life.' "

> —*DR. EVGENY CHAZOV*, representing
> International Physicians for the
> Prevention of Nuclear War   *(1985)*

"Physicians have demonstrated to the whole world
that not only would nuclear war spell the end of civilization, it would also prejudice the existence of life on
earth. My conscience—and I am sure the same applies
to many of my colleagues in IPPNW—was staggered,
primarily not by the total number of victims in nuclear
war. The human mind finds it difficult to comprehend
the figure of 2000 million victims. As they say, one
death is death, but a million deaths are statistics. For us
physicians, life is the aim of our work and each death is
a tragedy. As people constantly involved in the care of
patients, we felt the urge to warn governments and peoples that the critical point has been passed: medicine will
be unable to render even minimal assistance to the vic-

tims of a nuclear conflict—the wounded, the burned, the sick—including the population of the country which unleashes nuclear war."

—DR. EVGENY CHAZOV, representing
International Physicians for the
Prevention of Nuclear War *(1985)*

"This build-up is like a cancer, the cells of which multiply because they have been genetically programmed to do no other. Pointing nuclear-tipped missiles at entire nations is an unprecedented act of moral depravity. The horror is obscured by its magnitude, by the sophistication of the means of slaughter, and by the aseptic Orwellian language crafted to describe the attack—'delivery vehicles' promote an 'exchange' in which the death of untold millions is called 'collateral damage.' Bertrand Russell called attention to the ethical bankruptcy that afflicts this era: 'Our world has sprouted a weird concept of security and a warped sense of morality. Weapons are sheltered like treasures while children are exposed to incineration.' "

—DR. BERNARD LOWN, representing
International Physicians for the
Prevention of Nuclear War *(1985)*

"Nothing provokes so much horror and opposition within the Jewish tradition as war. Our abhorrence of war is reflected in the paucity of our literature of warfare. After all, God created the Torah to do away with iniquity, to do away with war. Warriors fare poorly in the Talmud: Judas Maccabaeus is not even mentioned; Bar-Kochba is cited, but negatively. David, a great warrior and conqueror, is not permitted to build the Temple; it is his son Solomon, a man of peace, who constructs God's dwelling place. Of course some wars may have been necessary or inevitable, but none was ever regarded as holy. For us, a holy war is a contradiction in terms. War dehumanizes, war diminishes, war debases all those who wage it. The Talmud says, *'Talmidei hakhamim shermarbin shalom baolam'* (It is the wise men who will bring about peace)."

—*ELIE WIESEL (1986)*

"We must remember the suffering of my people, as we must remember that of the Ethiopians, the Cambodians, the boat people, the Palestinians, the Mesquite Indians, the Argentinian *desaparecidos*—the list seems endless.

"Let us remember Job, who, having lost everything— his children, his friends, his possessions, and even his argument with God—still found the strength to begin again, to rebuild his life. Job was determined not to repudiate the creation, however imperfect, that God had entrusted to him."

—*ELIE WIESEL (1986)*

Oscar Arias Sánchez receiving an honorary degree from Harvard University (1988).

"The world today is divided between those who live in fear of being destroyed in nuclear war, and those who are dying day by day in wars fought with conventional weapons. This terror of the final war is so great that it has spread the most frightening insensibility towards the arms race and the use of non-nuclear weapons. We need most urgently—our intelligence requires us, our pity enjoins us—to struggle with equal intensity to ensure that neither Hiroshima nor Vietnam is repeated."

—*OSCAR ARIAS SÁNCHEZ* *(1987)*

"However noble a crusade, some people will desire and promote its failure. Some few appear to accept war as the normal course of events, as the solution to problems. How ironic that powerful forces are angered by interruptions in the course of war, by efforts to eliminate the sources of hatred! How ironic that any intention to stop war in its course triggers rages and attacks, as if we were disturbing the sleep of the just or halting a necessary measure, and not a heart-rending evil! How ironic for peacemaking efforts to discover that hatred is stronger for many than love; that the longing to achieve power through military victories makes so many men lose their reason, forget all shame, and betray history."

—*OSCAR ARIAS SÁNCHEZ* *(1987)*

Martin Luther King, Jr., (center, with button on lapel) *marching in Boston with Ralph Abernathy* (right) *and the Reverend Virgil Wood (1965).*

VIOLENCE
AND
NONVIOLENCE

"I believe the greatest risk of war is in the minds of men who have an unrepentant and unchanging view of the justification of past wars. So perhaps in a world like this there is room for a few thousand persons like Quakers, who take the opposite view, who begin with the assumption that war is not and has not been and will not be justified, on either practical or moral grounds."

—*HENRY J. CADBURY,* representing the American Friends Service Committee *(1947)*

"That does not mean that wars are not waged for just ends. It means that we do not believe that it is the only way to achieve those just ends. We believe the means are not consistent with the ends, and the better the ends for which men fight, the less moral, the less effective is the method of war. In this particular area, mankind falls behind the standard we have accepted elsewhere. So on this point the Quaker is not an unrealistic perfectionist, but a practical moralist. He believes that this problem can be solved by other means. He believes this problem of war is a moral problem and that the force of religion is essential to its solution. The nature of religion on the one hand and the task of abolishing war on the other seem to us to fit perfectly with each other as task and tool should fit. Religion is concerned with the spiritual life of man. The elimination of war is a spiritual problem and so no wonder we cling in all states of our religious development to this viewpoint."

—*HENRY J. CADBURY*, representing
the American Friends Service
Committee *(1947)*

"It has come to us first as individuals—what shall I do, what is my duty? If an individual thinks that war is evil, we are so simple-minded, so naive, as to say: 'If war is evil, then I do not take part in it,' just as one might say, if drunkenness is evil, then I do not drink; if slaveholding is evil, then I do not hold slaves. I know that sounds too simple—almost foolish. I admit that that is our point of view, and this means, of course, that in every war some Friends have suffered not only fines, torture, punishment, or exile, but even the threat of death, which, of course, is no more than the soldier faces, but in a different cause. . . . We recognize that there are times when resistance appears at first to be a real virtue, and then only those most deeply rooted in religious pacifism can resist by other than physical means. We have learned that in the end the spirit can conquer evil and we believe that in many recent situations those who have unwillingly employed force have learned this lesson at the last."

—*HENRY H. CADBURY*, representing
the American Friends Service
Committee *(1947)*

"I accept the Nobel Prize for Peace at a moment when 22 million Negroes of the United States of America are engaged in a creative battle to end the long night of racial injustice. I accept this award on behalf of a civil rights movement which is moving with determination and a majestic scorn for risk and danger to establish a reign of freedom and a rule of justice. I am mindful that only yesterday in Birmingham, Alabama, our children, crying out for brotherhood, were answered with fire hoses, snarling dogs and even death. I am mindful that only yesterday in Philadelphia, Mississippi, young people seeking to secure the right to vote were brutalized and murdered. And only yesterday more than forty houses of worship in the state of Mississippi alone were bombed or burned because they offered a sanctuary to those who would not accept segregation. I am mindful that debilitating and grinding poverty afflicts my people and chains them to the lowest rung of the economic ladder.

"Therefore, I must ask why this prize is awarded to a movement which is beleaguered and committed to unrelenting struggle: to a movement which has not won the very peace and brotherhood which is the essence of the Nobel Prize.

"After contemplation, I conclude that this award which I receive on behalf of that movement is a profound recognition that nonviolence is the answer to the crucial political and moral question of our time—the need for man to overcome oppression and violence without resorting to violence and oppression. Civilization and violence are antithetical concepts. Negroes of the United States, following the people of India, have demonstrated that nonviolence is not sterile passivity, but a powerful moral force which makes for social transforma-

tion. Sooner or later all the peoples of the world will have to discover a way to live together in peace, and thereby transform this pending cosmic elegy into a creative psalm of brotherhood. If this is to be achieved man must evolve for all human conflict a method which rejects revenge, aggression and retaliation. The foundation of such a method is love."
  —*MARTIN LUTHER KING, JR.* *(1964)*

"The word that symbolizes the spirit and the outward form of our encounter is nonviolence, and it is doubtless that factor which made it seem appropriate to award a peace prize to one identified with struggle. Broadly speaking, nonviolence in the civil rights struggle has meant not relying on arms and weapons of struggle. It has meant non-cooperation with customs and laws which are institutional aspects of a regime of discrimination and enslavement. . . .

"Nonviolence has also meant that my people in the agonizing struggles of recent years have taken suffering upon themselves instead of inflicting it on others."
  —*MARTIN LUTHER KING, JR.* *(1964)*

"In a real sense nonviolence seeks to redeem the spiritual and moral lag [that I spoke of earlier] as the chief dilemma of modern man. It seeks to secure moral ends through moral means. Nonviolence is a powerful and just weapon. Indeed, it is a weapon unique in history, which cuts without wounding and ennobles the man who wields it."

— *MARTIN LUTHER KING, JR.* *(1964)*

"We as Peace People go much further: we believe in taking down the barriers, but we also believe in the most energetic reconciliation among peoples by getting them to know each other, talk each other's languages, understand each other's fears and beliefs, getting to know each other physically, philosophically, and spiritually. It is much harder to kill your near neighbor than the thousands of unknown and hostile aliens at the other end of a nuclear missile. We have to create a world in which there are no unknown, hostile aliens at the other end of any missiles, and that is going to take a tremendous amount of sheer hard work.

"The only force which can break down those barriers is the force of love, the force of truth, soul-force. . . .

"We are deeply, passionately dedicated to the cause of nonviolence, to the force of truth and love, to soul-force. To those who say that we are naive, utopian idealists, we say that we are the only realists, and that those who continue to support militarism in our time are supporting the progress towards total self-destruction of the human race, when the only right and left will be dead to the right and dead to the left, and death and destruction right, left and center, east and west, north and south.

"We wish to see those who keep the lights burning twenty-four hours a day in the Pentagon and the Krem-

lin and all the other great centers of militarism liberated
into truly creative and happy lives instead of the soul-
destroying tasks of preparing for self-destruction."
—*BETTY WILLIAMS* *(1976)*

"I want to receive this distinction in the name of the
people of Latin America and, in a very special way, in
the name of the poorest and smallest of my brothers and
sisters because they are the most beloved of God. I receive it in the name of my indigenous brothers and sisters, the peasants, workers, and young people—in the
name of the thousands of members of religious orders
and of men and women of goodwill who relinquish their
privileges to share the life and path of the poor, and
who struggle to build a new society.

"For a man like myself—a small voice for those who
have no voice—who struggles so that the cry of the people may be heard in all its power; for one without any
identifying affiliation other than as a flesh-and-blood
Latin American and as a Christian, this is, without any
doubt, the highest honor that I can receive, which is to
be considered a servant of peace.

"I come from a continent that lives between anguish
and hope. For this continent where I live, the choice of
the evangelical power of nonviolence presents itself, I
am convinced, as a challenge that opens up new and radical perspectives.

"It is a choice that gives priority to a value essentially
and profoundly Christian—the dignity of the human
being, the sacred, transcendent, and irrevocable dignity

that belongs to the human being by reason of being a
child of God and a brother or sister in Christ, and therefore our own brother and sister."

—*ADOLFO PÉREZ ESQUIVEL (1980)*

"Because war and preparations for war have acquired
legitimacy, and because of the tremendous proliferation
of arms through production and export, so that they are
now available more or less to all and sundry, right down
to handguns and stilettoes, the cult of violence has by
now so permeated relations between people that we are
compelled to witness as well an increase in everyday
violence."

—*ALVA REIMER MYRDAL (1982)*

"War is murder. And the military preparations now
being made for a potential major conflict are aimed at
collective murder. In a nuclear age the victims would be
numbered by the millions.

"The naked truth of this must be faced.

"The age in which we live can only be described as
one of barbarism. Our civilization is in the process not
only of being militarized, but also of being brutalized.

"There are two main features characteristic of this
senseless trend: *rivalry* and *violence*. Rivalry for the
power to exploit the headlong onrush of technology
militates against cooperation, and results in increasing

violence, with more and more sophisticated weapons
being used. This is precisely what marks our age as one
of barbarism and brutalization. But the moment of truth
should now have arrived.

"I know that these are strong words. I know, too, that
there are good forces at work trying to check this ill-
starred development.

"May I at this juncture make a personal confession? I
have always regarded global development as a struggle
between good and evil forces. Not, to put it simply, a
struggle between Jesus and Satan, since I do not consider that the development is restricted to our own
sphere of culture. Rather perhaps a struggle between
Ormuzd, the good, and Ahriman, the evil. My personal
philosophy of life is *ethics*.

"It seems to me as if the evil forces have concentrated
more and more power in their hands. Dare we believe
that the leaders of the world's great nations will wake
up, will see the precipice towards which they are moving, and *change direction?*"

—*ALVA REIMER MYRDAL* (1982)

"When I recall my own path of life I cannot but speak
of the violence, hatred and lies. A lesson drawn from
such experiences, however, was that we can effectively
oppose violence only if we ourselves do not resort to it."

—*LECH WALESA* (1983)

"The technique which has come to be called peace-keeping uses soldiers as the servants of peace rather than as the instruments of war. It introduces to the military sphere the principle of nonviolence.

"Never before in history have military forces been employed internationally *not* to wage war, *not* to establish domination, and *not* to serve the interests of any power or group of powers, but rather to prevent conflict between peoples."

—*JAVIER PÉREZ DE CUÉLLAR,*
representing the United Nations
Peace-Keeping Forces *(1988)*

"The suffering of our people during the past forty years of occupation is well documented. Ours has been a long struggle. We know our cause is just. Because violence can only breed more violence and suffering, our struggle must remain nonviolent and free of hatred. We are trying to end the suffering of our people, not to inflict suffering upon others."

—*THE DALAI LAMA* *(1989)*

Andrei Sakharov participating in a protest against the Soviet Academy of Sciences (1989).

HUMAN
RIGHTS

"It is worthy of emphasis that the United Nations exists not merely to preserve the peace but also to make change—even radical change—possible without violent upheaval. The United Nations has no vested interest in the status quo. It seeks a more secure world, a better world, a world of progress for all peoples. In the dynamic world society which is the objective of the United Nations, all peoples must have equality and equal rights."

—*RALPH J. BUNCHE* (1950)

"The United Nations stands for the freedom and equality of all peoples, irrespective of race, religion, or ideology. It is for the peoples of every society to make their own choices with regard to ideologies, economic systems, and the relationship which is to prevail between the state and the individual. The United Nations is engaged in an historic effort to underwrite the rights of man. It is also attempting to give reassurance to the colonial peoples that their aspirations for freedom can be realized, if only gradually, by peaceful processes."

—*RALPH J. BUNCHE* (1950)

"Whatever may be the future of our freedom efforts, our cause is the cause of the liberation of people who are denied freedom. Only on this basis can the peace of Africa and the world be firmly founded. Our cause is the cause of equality between nations and peoples. Only thus can the brotherhood of man be firmly established."
—*ALBERT JOHN LUTULI (1960)*

"I did not initiate the struggle to extend the area of human freedom in South Africa; other African patriots—devoted men—did so before me. I also, as a Christian and patriot, could not look on while systematic attempts were made, almost in every department of life, to debase the God-factor in man or to set a limit beyond which the human being in his black form might not strive to serve his Creator to the best of his ability. To remain neutral in a situation where the laws of the land virtually criticized God for having created men of color was the sort of thing I could not, as a Christian, tolerate."
—*ALBERT JOHN LUTULI (1960)*

"The right of an individual to refuse to kill, to torture, or to participate in the preparation for the nuclear destruction of humanity seems to me to be fundamental."
—*SEAN MACBRIDE (1974)*

"I would like to end my speech expressing the hope in a final victory of the principles of peace and human rights. The best sign that such hope can come true would be a general political amnesty in all the world, liberation of all prisoners of conscience everywhere. The struggle for a general political amnesty is the struggle for the future of mankind.

"I am deeply grateful to the Nobel Committee for awarding me the Nobel Peace Prize for 1975 and I beg you to remember that the honor which was thus granted to me is shared by all prisoners of conscience in the Soviet Union and in other Eastern European countries as well as by all those who fight for their liberation."

—*ANDREI SAKHAROV* (1975)

"I am convinced that international confidence, mutual understanding, disarmament, and international security are inconceivable without an open society with freedom of information, freedom of conscience, the right to publish, and the right to travel and choose the country in which one wishes to live. I am likewise convinced that freedom of conscience, together with the other civic rights, provides the basis for scientific progress and constitutes a guarantee that scientific advances will not be used to despoil mankind, providing the basis for economic and social progress, which in turn is a political guarantee for the possibility of an effective defense of social rights. At the same time I should like to defend the thesis of the original and decisive significance of civic and political rights in molding the destiny of mankind.

This view differs essentially from the widely accepted
Marxist view, as well as the technocratic opinions, according to which it is precisely material factors and social
and economic conditions that are of decisive importance."

—*ANDREI SAKHAROV (1975)*

"Granting the award to a person who defends political
and civil rights against illegal and arbitrary actions means
an affirmation of principles which play such an important
role in determining the future of mankind. For hundreds
of people, known or unknown to me, many of whom
pay a high price for the defense of these same principles
(the price being loss of freedom, unemployment, poverty, persecution, exile from one's country), your decision was a great personal joy and a gift. I am aware of all
this, but I am also aware of another fact: in the present
situation, it is an act of intellectual courage and great
equity to grant the award to a man whose ideas do not
coincide with official concepts of the leadership of a big
and powerful state. This, in fact, is how I value the decision of the Nobel Committee; I also see in it a manifes-
tation of tolerance and of the true spirit of détente. I
want to hope that even those who at present view your
decision skeptically or with irritation someday will come
to share this point of view."

—*ANDREI SAKHAROV (1975)*

"People everywhere need to be continually reminded that violations of human rights, whether arbitrary arrest and detention, unjust imprisonment, torture, or political assassination, are threats to world peace. Each violation, wherever it occurs, can set in motion a trend towards the debasement of human dignity. From individuals to groups, from groups to nations, from nations to groups of nations, in chain reaction a pattern sets in, a pattern of violence and repression and a lack of concern for human welfare.

"This must never be allowed to start. And the place to stop it is at the level of the individual. Therefore, the protection of the rights of the individual to think freely, to express himself freely, to associate freely with others and to disseminate his thoughts is essential to the preservation of world peace."

—*MÜMTAZ SOYSAL,* representing
Amnesty International *(1977)*

"We are accustomed to hear, wherever human rights are being violated, that this is being done in the name of higher interests.

"I declare that there exists no higher interest than the Human Being.

"I point out my conviction of the maturity of the people, who are able to govern themselves without paternalistic guardians.

"For this reason we have hope. Because we believe in the vocation of communion and participation of our people, who day to day awaken to their political conscience and express their desire for change and profound democratization of society. A change based on justice, built with love, and which will bring to us the most anxiously desired fruits of peace.

"We must all commit ourselves to this task. And I want my voice to help build the chorus of voices so that the clamor for justice will become deafening.

"I live in the hope which I surely share with many others. I am confident that one day our daily effort will have its reward."

—*ADOLFO PÉREZ ESQUIVEL* (1980)

"In many parts of the world the people are searching for a solution which would link the two basic values: peace and justice. The two are like bread and salt for mankind."

—*LECH WALESA* (1983)

"You are aware of the reasons why I could not come to your capital city and receive personally this distinguished prize. On that solemn day my place is among those with whom I have grown and to whom I belong— the workers of Gdansk.

"Let my words convey to you the joy and the never extinguished hope of the millions of my brothers—the millions of working people in factories and offices, associated in the union whose very name expresses one of the noblest aspirations of humanity. Today all of them, like myself, feel greatly honored by the Prize. . . .

"For the first time a Pole has been awarded a prize which Alfred Nobel founded for activities towards bringing the nations of the world closer together.

"The most ardent hopes of my compatriots are linked with this idea—in spite of the violence, cruelty and brutality which characterize the conflicts splitting the present-day world.

"We desire peace—and that is why we have never resorted to physical force. We crave for justice—and that is why we are so persistent in the struggle for our rights. We seek freedom of convictions—and that is why we have never attempted to enslave man's conscience, nor shall we ever attempt to do so.

"We are fighting for the right of the working people to association and for the dignity of human labor. We respect the dignity and the rights of every man and every nation. The path to a brighter future of the world leads through honest reconciliation of the conflicting interests and not through hatred and bloodshed. To follow that path means to enhance the moral power of the all-embracing idea of human solidarity."

—*LECH WALESA*   (1983)

"One thing . . . must be said here and now on this solemn occasion: the Polish people have not been subjugated nor have they chosen the road of violence and fratricidal bloodshed.

"We shall not yield to violence. We shall not be de-

Lech Walesa at the Gdansk shipyard in Poland where the Solidarity trade union movement began (1983).

prived of union freedoms. We shall never agree with sending people to prison for their convictions. The gates of prisons must be thrown open and persons sentenced for defending union and civic rights must be set free. The announced trial of eleven leading members of our movement must never be held. All those already sentenced or still awaiting trials for their union activities or their convictions should return to their homes and be allowed to live and work in their country.

"The defense of our rights and our dignity, as well as efforts never to let ourselves be overcome by the feeling of hatred—this is the road we have chosen."

—*LECH WALESA* (1983)

"When will we learn that human beings are of infinite value because they have been created in the image of God, and that it is a blasphemy to treat them as if they were less than this, and to do so ultimately recoils on those who do this? In dehumanizing others, they are themselves dehumanized. Perhaps oppression dehumanizes the oppressor as much as, if not more than, the oppressed. They need each other to become truly free to become human. We can be human only in fellowship, in community, in *koinonia,* in peace."

—*DESMOND MPILO TUTU* (1984)

"It is with a profound sense of humility that I accept the honor you have chosen to bestow upon me. I know: your choice transcends me. This both frightens and pleases me.

"It frightens me because I wonder: do I have the right to represent the multitudes who have perished? Do I have the right to accept this great honor on their behalf? ... I do not. That would be presumptuous. No one may speak for the dead, no one may interpret their mutilated dreams and visions.

"It pleases me because I may say that this honor belongs to all the survivors and their children, and through us, to the Jewish people with whose destiny I have always identified."

—*ELIE WIESEL* (1986)

"I express to you my deepest gratitude. No one is as capable of gratitude as one who has emerged from the kingdom of night. We know that every moment is a moment of grace, every hour an offering; not to share them would mean to betray them. Our lives no longer belong to us alone; they belong to all those who need us desperately. . . .

"Thank you, people of Norway, for declaring on this singular occasion that our survival has meaning for mankind."

—*ELIE WIESEL* (1986)

"I swore never to be silent whenever and wherever human beings endure suffering and humiliation. We must always take sides. Neutrality helps the oppressor, never the victim. Silence encourages the tormentor, never the tormented. Sometimes we must interfere. When human lives are endangered, when human dignity is in jeopardy, national borders and sensitivities become irrelevant. Wherever men or women are persecuted because of their race, religion, or political views, that place must—at that moment—become the center of the universe."

—*ELIE WIESEL* *(1986)*

"There is much to be done, there is much that can be done. One person—a Raoul Wallenberg, an Albert Schweitzer, one person of integrity—can make a difference, a difference of life and death. As long as one dissident is in prison, our freedom will not be true. As long as one child is hungry, our lives will be filled with anguish and shame. What all these victims need above all is to know that they are not alone; that we are not forgetting them, that when their voices are stifled we shall lend them ours, that while their freedom depends on ours, the quality of our freedom depends on theirs."

—*ELIE WIESEL* *(1986)*

"Job, our ancestor. Job, our contemporary. His ordeal concerns all humanity. Did he ever lose his faith? If so, he rediscovered it within his rebellion. He demonstrated that faith is essential to rebellion, and that hope is possible beyond despair. The source of his hope was memory, as it must be ours. Because I remember, I despair. Because I remember, I have the duty to reject despair.

"I remember the killers, I remember the victims, even as I struggle to invent a thousand and one reasons to hope.

"There may be times when we are powerless to prevent injustice, but there must never be a time when we fail to protest. The Talmud tells us that by saving a single human being, man can save the world. We may be powerless to open all the jails and free all the prisoners, but by declaring our solidarity with one prisoner, we indict all jailers. None of us is in a position to eliminate war, but it is our obligation to denounce it and expose it in all its hideousness. . . . Mankind needs peace more than ever, for our entire planet, threatened by nuclear war, is in danger of total destruction. A destruction only man can provoke, only man can prevent.

"Mankind must remember that peace is not God's gift to his creatures, it is our gift to each other."

—*ELIE WIESEL* *(1986)*

"When you decided to honor me with this prize, you decided to honor a country of peace, you decided to honor Costa Rica. When, in this year 1987, you carried out the will of Alfred Nobel to encourage peace efforts in the world, you decided to encourage the efforts to secure peace in Central America. I am very grateful for the recognition of our search for peace. . . .

"To receive this Nobel Prize on the 10th of December is for me a marvelous coincidence. My son—here present—is eight years old today. I say to him, and through him to all the children of my country, that we shall never resort to violence, we shall never support military solutions to the problems of Central America. It is for the new generation that we must understand more than ever that this can only be achieved through its own instruments: dialogue and understanding, tolerance and forgiveness, freedom and democracy.

"I know well you share what we say to all members of the international community, and particularly to those both in the East and West with far greater power and resources than my small nation could ever hope to possess. I say to them with the utmost urgency, let Central Americans decide the future of Central America; leave interpretation, implementation of our peace plan to us. Support the efforts for peace instead of the forces of war in our region. Send our peoples ploughshares instead of swords, pruning hooks instead of shears. If they, for their own purposes, cannot refrain from amassing the weapons of war, then in the name of God, at least they should leave us in peace."

—*OSCAR ARIAS SÁNCHEZ* *(1987)*

"Costa Rica's fortress, the strength which makes it invincible by force, which makes it stronger than a thousand armies, is the power of liberty, of its principles, of the great ideals of our civilization."

—*OSCAR ARIAS SÁNCHEZ* *(1987)*

"As a free spokesman for my captive countrymen and -women, I feel it is my duty to speak out on their behalf. I speak not with a feeling of anger or hatred towards those who are responsible for the immense suffering of our people and the destruction of our land, homes and culture. They too are human beings who struggle to find happiness and deserve our compassion. I speak to inform you of the sad situation in my country today and of the aspirations of my people, because in our struggle for freedom, truth is the only weapon we possess."

—*THE DALAI LAMA* *(1989)*

Willy Brandt at his mayor's office in West Berlin (1958).

POLITICS
AND
LEADERSHIP

"The grim fact, however, is that we prepare for war like precocious giants and for peace like retarded pygmies."

—*LESTER B. PEARSON* (1957)

"Nansen was the first to say what others have repeated, that 'the difficult is what takes a little while; the impossible is what takes a little longer.' If politics is the art of the possible, statesmanship is the art, in Nansen's sense, of the impossible; and it is statesmanship that our perplexed and tortured humanity requires today."

—*PHILIP NOEL-BAKER* (1959)

"I do not feel like making loud appeals, for it is easy to demand moderation, reason and modesty of others. But this plea comes from the bottom of my heart: May all those who possess the power to wage war have the mastery of reason to maintain peace."

—*WILLY BRANDT* (1971)

"I pay no attention to those doubters and detractors unwilling to believe that a lasting peace can be genuinely embraced by those who march under a different ideological banner or those who are more accustomed to cannons of war than to councils of peace.

"We seek in Central America not peace alone, not peace to be followed someday by political progress, but peace and democracy, together, indivisible, an end to the shedding of human blood, which is inseparable from an end to the suppression of human rights. We do not judge, much less condemn, any other nation's political or ideological system, freely chosen and never exported. We cannot require sovereign states to conform to patterns of government not of their own choosing. But we can and do insist that every government respect those universal rights of man that have meaning beyond national boundaries and ideological labels. We believe that justice and peace can only thrive together, never apart. A nation that mistreats its own citizens is more likely to mistreat its neighbors."

—*OSCAR ARIAS SÁNCHEZ (1987)*

"I come from a world with huge problems, which we shall overcome in freedom. I come from a world in a hurry, because hunger cannot wait. When hope is forgotten, violence does not delay. Dogmatism is too impatient for dialogue. . . . I come from a world which cannot wait for the guerrilla and the soldier to hold their fire: young people are dying, brothers are dying, and tomorrow who can tell why. I come from a world which cannot wait to open prison gates not, as before, for free men to go in, but for those imprisoned to come out.

"America's liberty and democracy have no time to lose, and we need the whole world's understanding to win freedom from dictators, to win freedom from misery.

"I come from Central America.

"I accept this prize as one of 27 million Central Americans. Behind the democratic awakening in Central America lies over a century of merciless dictatorships and general injustice and poverty. The choice before my little America is whether to suffer another century of violence, or to achieve peace by overcoming the fear of liberty. Only peace can write the new history."
—*OSCAR ARIAS SÁNCHEZ* (1987)

"History can only move towards liberty. History can only have justice at its heart. To march in the opposite direction to history is to be on the road to shame, poverty and oppression. Without freedom, there is no revolution. All oppression runs counter to man's spirit."
—*OSCAR ARIAS SÁNCHEZ* (1987)

BIOGRAPHICAL NOTES

The following biographical entries include only those prize winners whose speeches and lectures have been excerpted for this volume. For a listing of all of the prize winners, the reader may refer to the Chronology on pages 137–38.

Note: The italicized date in each entry represents the year for which the prize was awarded; on several occasions the Nobel Committee postponed its decision for a certain year and then made the grant of that year's prize one year later.

AMERICAN FRIENDS SERVICE COMMITTEE of the United States and the **FRIENDS SERVICE COUNCIL** of Great Britain. *1947.* HENRY J. CADBURY and MARGARET BACKHOUSE, respectively, represented these Quaker organizations, awarded the Nobel Peace Prize for their relief and reconstruction work during and after World War II.

AMNESTY INTERNATIONAL (1961–). *1977.* This international organization that defends the rights of prisoners of conscience was represented at the award ceremony by its chairman, THOMAS HAMMARBERG of Sweden, who gave the acceptance speech, and its vice-chairman, MÜMTAZ SOYSAL of Turkey, who delivered the lecture.

ANGELL, NORMAN (1872–1967). *1933.* British author of the noted peace book *The Great Illusion,* who served the cause for many years as a very influential publicist and lecturer.

ARIAS SÁNCHEZ, OSCAR (1941–   ). *1987.* President of Costa Rica, a democratic country without an army, who succeeded in gaining the approval of the four other presidents of the region for his peace plan for Central America. The Nobel Committee hoped that its prize would aid his efforts.

ARNOLDSON, KLAS PONTUS (1844–1916). *1908.* Sweden's leading peace activist. Inspired by his liberal Christianity, he served the peace cause as a politician, organizer, and influential orator and publicist.

BACKHOUSE, MARGARET. See American Friends Service Committee of the United States.

BALCH, EMILY GREENE (1867–1961). *1946.* Scholar and intellectual leader of the American peace movement. With Jane Addams (1931) she was a cofounder of the Women's International League for Peace and Freedom, for which she worked many years in Geneva and in the United States.

BEGIN, MENACHEM (1913–   ), and **MOHAMMED ANWAR EL-SADAT** (1918–81). *1978.* Prime Minister of Israel and President of the Arab Republic of Egypt, given the prize for their agreement at Camp David, where they had been brought together by President Jimmy Carter, to end the state of war between their two countries that had lasted for thirty years. Sadat's peace policy was criticized by many Egyptians and by other Arab states, and he decided not to appear with Begin at Oslo but to send his counselor SAYED MAREI to read his speech of acceptance. The award ceremony was moved to the Akershus fortress to provide more security for Begin, when he delivered his own acceptance speech.

BORLAUG, NORMAN (1914–). *1970*. American agricultural scientist whose impact on the increased production of wheat, maize, and rice earned him the title "father of the Green Revolution." In the words of the Nobel Committee: "More than any other single person in this age, he has helped to provide bread for a hungry world. We have made this choice in the hope that providing bread will also give the world peace."

BOURGEOIS, LÉON (1851–1925). *1920*. French political leader who helped prepare the way for the establishment of the League of Nations, both in his writings and throughout his political career. He chaired the French delegation at both intergovernmental peace conferences at The Hague and helped write the Covenant of the League at the Paris Peace Conference. Ill and unable to attend the award ceremony, Bourgeois sent a "Communication" to the Nobel Committee in December 1922, from which these excerpts are taken.

BOYD-ORR OF BRECHIN, LORD (1880–1971). *1949*. John Boyd-Orr was a Scottish medical doctor and nutritionist, a founder and director general of the United Nations Food and Agricultural Organization and later a prominent international peace leader.

BRANDT, WILLY (1913–). *1971*. The second German statesman to be honored for his policy of peace and reconciliation with former enemy states. As foreign minister and chancellor of the Federal Republic, Brandt strengthened ties with Western European states and negotiated peace pacts with Poland and the Soviet Union. After leaving office, he continued to work for peace as a leader of the world's Social Democrats.

BUNCHE, RALPH J. (1904–71). *1950.* American social scientist who served as a State Department official and then as a top UN administrator. As UN mediator, he negotiated the ending of the Arab-Jewish hostilities over Palestine in 1949.

CADBURY, HENRY J. See American Friends Service Committee of the United States.

CHAPUISAT, ÉDOUARD. See International Committee of the Red Cross.

CHAZOV, DR. EVGENY. See International Physicians for the Prevention of Nuclear War.

DALAI LAMA XIV of Tibet, **TENZIN GYATSO** (1935–). *1989.* Enthroned in 1940 as the spiritual and temporal ruler of Tibet, he went into exile in India in 1959, after the Chinese, who regard Tibet as part of China, sent in their army to establish control. Since then he has worked untiringly from abroad to liberate his people. He was given the prize for this championing of human rights by the means of nonviolence, for his Buddhist message of love and compassion, and for his efforts to awaken concern for the environment.

FRIENDS SERVICE COUNCIL of Great Britain. See American Friends Service Committee of the United States.

HARTLING, POUL. See Office of the United Nations High Commissioner for Refugees.

HENDERSON, ARTHUR (1863–1935). *1934.* British foreign secretary known for his peace policies and his strong support of the League of Nations. As president of the World Disarmament Conference (1932–35), he worked valiantly but in vain to make it a success.

INTERNATIONAL COMMITTEE OF THE RED CROSS. *1944.* At the award ceremony held in December 1945 MAX HUBER, honorary president, accepted the prize in behalf of the ICRC, the second of the three which this Swiss organization has received. ÉDOUARD CHAPUISAT, a member of the ICRC, gave the Nobel lecture. See The League of Red Cross Societies for the 1963 award.

INTERNATIONAL PHYSICIANS FOR THE PRE-VENTION OF NUCLEAR WAR (IPPNW) (1980–   ). *1985.* DR. EVGENY CHAZOV of the Soviet Union and DR. BERNARD LOWN of the United States were invited by the Nobel Committee to receive the prize as copresidents of IPPNW, an international federation with members in forty countries. The Nobel Committee had been impressed both with the message of IPPNW that there could be no adequate medical response to nuclear warfare and with the cooperation of Soviet and American physicians.

KING, MARTIN LUTHER, JR. (1929–68). *1964.* The leader of the nonviolent movement for civil rights in the United States. A Baptist minister who had undertaken advanced studies, his sermons and speeches are considered among the best examples of American oratory. The chairman of the Norwegian Nobel Committee declared: "He is the first person in the Western world to have shown us that a struggle can be waged without violence. He is the first to make the message of brotherly love a reality in the course of his struggle, and he has brought this message to all men, to all nations and races."

LANGE, CHRISTIAN L. (1869–1938). *1921.* A leading Norwegian internationalist, both as a scholar and as the longtime secretary-general of the Interparliamentary Union and a member of the Norwegian delegation to the Assembly of the League of Nations.

THE LEAGUE OF RED CROSS SOCIETIES. *1963.* In this centenary year of the founding of the Red Cross, the League shared the prize with the **INTERNATIONAL COMMITTEE OF THE RED CROSS.** JOHN A. MACAULAY, the Canadian jurist who was chairman of the board of governors of the League in Geneva, delivered the Nobel lecture in its behalf.

LOWN, DR. BERNARD. See International Physicians for the Prevention of Nuclear War.

LUTULI, ALBERT JOHN (1898–1967). *1960.* Zulu tribal chief in South Africa, president of the African National Congress, and leader in the nonviolent struggle against the policies of apartheid.

MacAULAY, JOHN A. See The League of Red Cross Societies.

MacBRIDE, SEAN (1904–88). *1974.* Once an Irish revolutionary and always a passionate nationalist, MacBride became a strong internationalist who was honored with the Peace Prize for his championship of human rights. As Irish foreign minister, he gained the approval of the Council of Europe for the European Convention on Human Rights. He helped found Amnesty International (1977), as a lawyer promoted human rights through the International Commission of Jurists, and held top positions in various international peace organizations.

MARSHALL, GEORGE C. (1880–1959). *1953.* General Marshall served the United States for many years as an army officer, finally as chief of staff during World War II, making a most important contribution to the victory. He served also as secretary of state and of defense. In the former position his "Marshall Plan" of economic assistance brought about the reconstruction of Europe's economy after the war. For this he was awarded the Peace Prize.

MONETA, ERNESTO TEODORO (1830–1918). *1907.* Journalist and editor who headed the Italian peace movement. In his youth Moneta had taken part in the struggle for unification of his country, and he hoped for a peace based upon fraternal relationships between peoples who had achieved their freedom and national unity.

MYRDAL, ALVA REIMER (1902–86). *1982.* Swedish social reformer, cabinet minister, and diplomat, co-winner with **ALFONSO GARCÍA ROBLES,** former Mexican foreign minister, for their efforts to promote disarmament. Both had been prominent in the disarmament discussions at the UN, Myrdal as Sweden's top disarmament negotiator and author of widely discussed works on the subject. A member of the upper chamber of parliament, she served in the cabinet for twelve years and was known as the "Grand Old Lady of Swedish Politics." She was married to Gunnar Myrdal, Nobel laureate in economics.

NANSEN, FRIDTJOF (1861–1930). *1922.* Famous Arctic explorer and diplomat of Norway, who directed the refugee programs of the League of Nations and other relief work after World War I.

NOEL-BAKER, PHILIP (1889–1982). *1959.* British Quaker politician and cabinet minister, who played a role in the establishment of both the League of Nations and the United Nations and was a lifelong champion of disarmament.

OFFICE OF THE UNITED NATIONS HIGH COMMISSIONER FOR REFUGEES (1951–). *1954.* At the award ceremony Dr. G. JAN VAN HEUVEN GOEDHART of the Netherlands, the High Commissioner, represented his organization, whose work for the uprooted and the homeless, the chairman of the Norwegian Nobel Committee declared, promoted brotherhood among men. See below for the 1981 award.

OFFICE OF THE UNITED NATIONS HIGH COMMISSIONER FOR REFUGEES (1951–). *1981.* Accepting the second prize for this agency was its high commissioner, POUL HARTLING of Denmark, who delivered the lecture.

PAULING, LINUS (1901–). *1962.* Only winner of two undivided Nobel prizes, for chemisty and peace. Awarded the Peace Prize for his mobilization of the scientists of the world in a protest against nuclear testing in the atmosphere, which helped bring about the partial Test Ban Treaty concluded in 1963, the year when Pauling received the postponed prize of 1962.

PEARSON, LESTER B. (1897–1972). *1957.* Canadian diplomat and foreign minister, responsible for the establishment of the UN Emergency Force, through which the Suez conflict of 1956 was brought to an end.

PÉREZ DE CUÉLLAR, JAVIER. See The United Nations Peace-Keeping Forces.

PÉREZ ESQUIVEL, ADOLFO (1931–). *1980.* A leader in the Latin American nonviolent movement for human rights, who left his position as a teacher of art in Argentina to become the secretary-general of its organization Service for Peace and Justice. Although he was a devout Catholic who opposed acts of violence of the Left as well as of the Right, the military government of Argentina treated him as a subversive and he was subjected to imprisonment and torture.

PIRE, FATHER DOMINIQUE (1910–69). *1958.* Belgian Dominican priest, who was given the prize "for his efforts to help refugees leave their camps and return to a life of freedom." One project was to build communities of small houses ("villages") next to cities, where the refugees could be integrated in society. Pire was especially concerned with the "Hard Core," the refugees who were old or infirm and often disregarded by other refugee agencies.

SADAT, MOHAMMED ANWAR EL-. See Begin, Menachem.

SAKHAROV, ANDREI (1921–89). *1975.* Honored by the Nobel Committee as "one of the great champions of human rights in our age," Sakharov was the scientific genius celebrated in the Soviet Union for his role in developing the Soviet hydrogen bomb who became a critic of government policies and courageously asked for liberalization of Soviet society. As the country's leading dissident, Sakharov was persecuted and refused permission to travel to Oslo to receive the prize. But his wife, Yelena Bonner, was already abroad to receive medical treatment and was able to read his acceptance speech and his Nobel lecture at Oslo.

SATO, EISAKU (1901–75). *1974.* Longtime premier of Japan, given the prize after leaving office for his peaceful foreign policy in Asia and for securing Japan's adherence to the nuclear proliferation treaty.

SCHWEITZER, ALBERT (1875–1965). *1952.* Born in the French province of Alsace, recently annexed by the German Empire, Schweitzer was a many-sided genius who could have followed a distinguished career in philosophy, theology, or music, in each of which fields he received a doctorate. Instead, he then trained as a doctor and spent the rest of his life as a medical missionary in the African jungle, putting into practice his convictions about human brotherhood.

SÖDERBLOM, NATHAN (1866–1931). *1930.* As Archbishop of Uppsala and the top prelate of Sweden, he took world leadership in working for peace through the ecumenical movement.

SOYSAL, MÜMTAZ. See Amnesty International.

STRESEMANN, GUSTAV (1878–1929). *1926.* German statesman who, with laureates Aristide Briand of France and Austen Chamberlain of Great Britain, negotiated the treaties of reconciliation among the former enemy states of World War I.

SUTTNER, BERTHA VON (1843–1914). *1905.* The Austrian baroness who wrote the famous antiwar novel *Lay Down Your Arms* and became a major leader of the organized peace movement. She influenced her friend Alfred Nobel in his decision to establish the Peace Prize.

TERESA, MOTHER (1910–   ). *1979.* Known as the "Saint of Calcutta" for her works of mercy for the poor in its slums. Born to an Albanian family in what is now Yugoslav Macedonia, she joined a Catholic teaching order to serve in its missionary school in Calcutta, but overwhelmed by the poverty and misery she found there, she heeded the call to leave the convent and to help the poor while living among them. As she cared for the hungry, the sick, and the dying, others joined her, and she founded a new order, the Missionaries of Charity, whose good works have reached far beyond India to centers of need all over the world.

TUTU, DESMOND MPILO (1931–   ). *1984.* Anglican church leader who was given the prize for his nonviolent struggle against apartheid in South Africa. First a teacher, then an Anglican priest who studied theology in England, Tutu became a bishop and then general secretary of the South African Council of Churches, leading these churches in a campaign against apartheid as contrary to the teachings of Christianity. He later became Archbishop of Cape Town and head of the Anglican Church of South Africa.

THE UNITED NATIONS PEACE-KEEPING FORCES. *1988.* Accepting the prize for the "Blue Berets" was their commander, JAVIER PÉREZ DE CUÉLLAR, Secretary-General of the United Nations, flanked on either side of the stage by a line of these "soldiers of peace," who had been flown to Oslo for the occasion from their posts around the world. They represented more than ten thousand UN peace-keepers then on duty, stationed as a buffer between hostile forces or monitoring truce agreements. To the chairman of the Nobel Committee the peace-keeping forces, composed of contingents from many countries, were "a tangible expression of the world community's will to solve conflicts by peaceful means."

VAN HEUVEN GOEDHART, DR. G. JAN. See Office of the United Nations High Commissioner for Refugees.

WALESA, LECH (1943–   ). *1983.* Polish worker who became head of Solidarity, the free trade union movement.

The struggle to establish workers' rights and a freer society met with government repression, and Walesa and other leaders were arrested. Although released before the announcement of his prize, Walesa decided not to go to Oslo, fearing that the government would not permit him to return. He sent his wife, Danuta, to receive the prize, and she read his speech of acceptance. A Solidarity comrade read Walesa's Nobel lecture, which was then read in Norwegian translation by a well-known actor.

WIESEL, ELIE (1928–). *1986.* Jewish survivor of the Holocaust, born in Romania, now an American citizen. An eloquent author and speaker, honored by the Nobel Committee for his tireless efforts as spokesman for those who died to keep their memory alive and to defend victims of inhumanity everywhere so that such a tragedy would never happen again. "In him," declared the Nobel Committee chairman, "we see a man who has climbed from utter humiliation to become one of our most important spiritual leaders and guides."

WILLIAMS [PERKINS], BETTY (1943–). *1976.* Co-winner with **MAIREAD CORRIGAN [MAGUIRE]** (1944–), two young women of simple backgrounds in Belfast, Northern Ireland, who founded the Peace People, a nonviolent movement to reconcile Catholics and Protestants and stop the killing in that troubled province of Great Britain. Williams gave the lecture in behalf of both laureates at the award ceremony in 1977.

CHRONOLOGY

Year	Laureate
1901	H. Dunant (Switzerland)
	F. Passy (France)
1902	E. Ducommun (Switzerland)
	A. Gobat (Switzerland)
1903	W.R. Cremer (Great Britain)
1904	Institute for Int'l Law, Ghent
1905	Bertha von Suttner (Austria)
1906	T. Roosevelt (U.S.)
1907	E. T. Moneta (Italy)
	L. Renault (France)
1908	K. P. Arnoldson (Sweden)
	F. Bajer (Denmark)
1909	A. M. F. Beernaert (Belgium)
	P. H. d'Estournelles-de Constant (France)
1910	Int'l Peace Bureau, Bern
1911	T. M. C. Asser (Netherlands)
	A. H. Fried (Austria)
1912	Elihu Root (U.S.)
1913	H. La Fontaine (Belgium)
1914	None
1915	None
1916	None
1917	Int'l Red Cross, Geneva
1918	None
1919	T. W. Wilson (U.S.)
1920	L. Bourgeois (France)
1921	K. H. Branting (Sweden)
	C. L. Lange (Norway)

Year	Laureate
1922	F. Nansen (Norway)
1923	None
1924	None
1925	C. G. Dawes (U.S.)
	A. Chamberlain (Great Britain)
1926	A. Briand (France)
	G. Stresemann (Germany)
1927	F. Buisson (France)
	L. Quidde (Germany)
1928	None
1929	F. B. Kellogg (U.S.)
1930	N. Söderblom (Sweden)
1931	N. M. Butler (U.S.)
	J. Addams (U.S.)
1932	None
1933	N. Angell (Great Britain)
1934	A. Henderson (Great Britain)
1935	C. von Ossietzky (Germany)
1936	C. Saavedra Lamas (Argentina)
1937	E. A. R. G. Cecil (Great Britain)
1938	Nansen Int'l Office for Refugees, Geneva
1939	None
1940	None
1941	None
1942	None
1943	None
1944	Int'l Committee of the Red Cross, Geneva
1945	C. Hull (U.S.)

Year	Laureate	Year	Laureate
1946	E. G. Balch (U.S.)	1970	N. E. Borlaug (U.S.)
	J. R. Mott (U.S.)	1971	W. Brandt (Germany)
1947	The Friends Service	1972	None
	Council (Great Britain)	1973	H. A. Kissinger (U.S.)
	The American Friends		[Le Duc Tho (N.
	Service Committee		Vietnam) (declined the
	(U.S.)		prize)]
1948	None	1974	S. MacBride (Ireland)
1949	J. Boyd-Orr (Great		E. Sato (Japan)
	Britain)	1975	A. Sakharov (U.S.S.R.)
1950	R. J. Bunche (U.S.)	1976	M. Corrigan (Great
1951	L. Jouhaux (France)		Britain)
1952	A. Schweitzer (France)		B. Williams (Great
1953	G. C. Marshall (U.S.)		Britain)
1954	Office of the UN High	1977	Amnesty Int'l
	Commissioner for	1978	M. Begin (Israel)
	Refugees, Geneva		A. Sadat (Egypt)
1955	None	1979	Mother Teresa (India)
1956	None	1980	A. Pérez Esquivel
1957	L. B. Pearson (Canada)		(Argentina)
1958	G. Pire (Belgium)	1981	Office of the High
1959	P. J. Noel-Baker (Great		Commissioner for
	Britain)		Refugees, Geneva
1960	A. J. Lutuli (South	1982	A. Myrdal (Sweden)
	Africa)		A. García Robles
1961	D. Hammarskjöld		(Mexico)
	(Sweden)	1983	L. Waiesa (Poland)
1962	L. C. Pauling (U.S.)	1984	D. Tutu (South Africa)
1963	Int'l Committee of the	1985	Int'l Physicians for the
	Red Cross, Geneva		Prevention of Nuclear
	League of Red Cross		War
	Societies, Geneva	1986	E. Wiesel (U.S.)
1964	M. L. King (U.S.)	1987	O. Arias Sánchez (Costa
1965	UN Children's Fund		Rica)
	(UNICEF)	1988	UN Peace-Keeping
1966	None		Forces
1967	None	1989	The Dalai Lama XIV
1968	R. Cassin (France)		(Tibet)
1969	Int'l Labor Organization,		
	Geneva		

INDEX

Page numbers in *italics* refer to photographs.

THE ACCLAIMED NEWMARKET *WORDS OF* SERIES

Ideal introductions to the thoughts, feelings, and personalities of the century's most vibrant, vi
people, presented in beautifully designed, illustrated gift editions.

The Words of Peace
Selections from the Speeches of the Winners of the Nobel Peace Prize
Edited by Professor Irwin Abrams. Foreword by President Jimmy Carter.
A new compendium of excerpts from the award winners' acceptance speeches from 1901 to
1990, including the Dalai Lama, Mother Teresa, Lech Walesa, Martin Luther King, Jr., and Eli
Wiesel. Themes are: Peace, Human Rights, Violence and Nonviolence, the Bonds of Humanit
Faith and Hope, plus much more.

The Words of Desmond Tutu
Selected and introduced by Naomi Tutu
Nearly 100 memorable quotations from the addresses, sermons, and writings of South Africa's
Nobel Prize-winning Archbishop. Topics include: Faith and Responsibility, Apartheid, Family,
Violence and Nonviolence, The Community—Black and White, and Toward a New South Af
10 photographs; chronology; text of acceptance speech for the Nobel Peace Prize, 1984.

The Words of Martin Luther King, Jr.
Selected and introduced by Coretta Scott King
Over 120 quotations and excerpts from the great civil rights leader's speeches, sermons, and
writings on: The Community of Man, Racism, Civil Rights, Justice and Freedom, Faith and
Religion, Nonviolence, and Peace. 16 photos; chronology; text of presidential proclamation
of King holiday.

The Words of Martin Luther King, Jr. Calendar
Quotations from letters, speeches, and writings, illustrated with inspirational, historical
photographs. Highlights important events in Dr. King's life, North American holidays and
astronomical data. For all ages. 10 x 12. 13 photos. Published annually.

The Words of Gandhi
Selected and introduced by Richard Attenborough
Over 150 selections from the letters, speeches, and writings collected in five sections—Daily
Life, Cooperation, Nonviolence, Faith, and Peace.

The Words of Albert Schweitzer
Selected and introduced by Norman Cousins
An inspiring collection focusing on: Knowledge and Discovery, Reverence for Life, Faith,
The Life of the Soul, The Musician as Artist, and Civilization and Peace.

More Inspirational Biography
Gandhi: A Pictorial Biography
Text by Gerald Gold. Photo selection and Afterword by Richard Attenborough.
The important personal, political and spiritual periods of Gandhi's life. "First Rate."—LA Time

Newmarket Press books are available from your local bookseller or from Newmarket Press, 18
East 48th Street, New York, New York 10017, (212) 832-3575. Catalogs and ordering
information are available on request.